ST. PAUL, OREGON
1830-1890

ST. PAUL, OREGON
1830-1890

by

Harvey J. McKay

Binford & Mort

Thomas Binford, Publisher

2536 S.E. Eleventh • Portland, Oregon 97202

Dedication

To my father and mother,
Arthur W. McKay and Grace (Murphy) McKay,
and all the other people who lived in
the St. Paul area between 1830 and 1890

and

to their descendants

St. Paul, Oregon, 1830-1890

Copyright © 1980 by Harvey James McKay

Printed in the United States of America

Library of Congress Catalog Card Number:80-69228
ISBN: 0-8323-0384-4

First Edition 1980

FOREWORD

With the completion of the Louisiana Purchase by President Jefferson in 1803, the development of a new civilization became inevitable for the land between the Mississippi River and the Pacific Ocean. But the change was not to come easily.

Lewis and Clark, in their search for a northwest water passage across this vast unknown land, found that because of the high mountains and river filled with giant rocks and tortuous rapids, no water passage existed. Moreover, the obstacles to a land passage were almost insurmountable.

When Lewis and Clark, with the invaluable assistance furnished by the fabled Sacagewea and her various Indian contacts, completed the nineteen-month, 2,500-mile journey from St. Louis, Missouri, to the mouth of the Columbia River, they knew that only strong men and women would be able to complete the hazardous journey which was necessary to get to the faraway land bordering on the Pacific Ocean.

Despite the great difficulties which were known to exist, a few fur trappers were able to surmount them. Later, but very gradually, small groups of people, which sometimes included a few women, successfully met the almost unbelievable challenges and arrived at a new home in the remote wilderness. Eventually, people were to come in organized wagon trains and find a shorter route which became known as the Oregon Trail; but the 2,000-mile journey, which took six months, remained almost as challenging as it had been for those who first made the crossing.

In 1869, sixty-four years after Lewis and Clark made the first crossing, the trip across the great plains and the Rocky Mountains was changed dramatically when the transcontinental railroad was completed. But by this time the character of the Far West had been firmly established by people who had come by horseback or covered wagon and had apparently learned to enjoy meeting and overcoming great challenges.

In any momentous event there are particular locales that are destined to play key roles. The subject of this book, St. Paul, Oregon, because of its strategic location at the time and because of its adjacent fertile prairies in a mostly timbered land, played an important part in the development of a new civilization in a then faraway land.

This book is an attempt to tell the authentic story of this historically important community, St. Paul, Oregon, and the people who lived there during the 1830-1890 period.

ACKNOWLEDGMENTS

I began this project in early 1975, not realizing its magnitude or the amount of research that would be necessary to ensure that the book would come close to representing St. Paul as it really was in the 1830-1890 period. It would have been a much easier task if it had been attempted seventy-five years ago. The book is the result of the cooperation of many people—it could truthfully be called a community project.

The task began when I contacted representatives of the early-day St. Paul families and advised them of the proposal to write a history of the community. All agreed that the area had been historically significant and, inasmuch as a history of the community had never been written, they would be more than happy to particiapte in the effort. The families generally felt that it would be a valuable contribution to Oregon history and that even though the project would be difficult, because of the passage of time, it would be worthwhile.

Six individuals who descended from families which came to St. Paul before 1860, and who grew up in the St. Paul area in the 1890's, provided invaluable assistance by furnishing information, verifying other information, and, in general, contributing a feeling of what St. Paul was really like during the 1830-1890 period. They are Frank "Babe" Jette, Charles "Charley" Mullen, Geraldine Kirk, Sr. Estelle, S.N.J.M. (Estelle McKay), John Gearin and F. Rosswell "Ross" Coleman.

Bishop Francis P. Leipsig, historian for the Catholic Archdiocese of Portland in Oregon, and Sister Ann Harold, historian for the Congregation of the Sisters of the Holy Names, furnished records of the Church and Catholic schools in the St. Paul area and other related information.

A.D. "Scotty" Graham of Salem obtained the official 1852 United States Government maps shown.

Thirty-two individuals furnished short histories of their families and some of the other information contained in this book. They are Albert Belleque, Harold Brentano, Agnes (Buyserie) McKay, Delight (McHale) Lorenz, F. Rosswell "Ross" Coleman, Margaret "Peggy" (Connor)

Bergquist, Eugenia "Jean" (Cooke) Abner, Ardis (Clark) LeFevre, Alice Davidson, Norman "Mutt" Ernst, Dr. John Gearin, Elmer "Sam" Gooding, Alicia (Smith) Koch, Frank "Babe" Jette, Charles and Patrick Johnston, Clarence Kavanaugh, Mabel (Smith) Lampkin, Lucille (Kennedy) Sturgeon, Geraldine Kirk, Louis Labonte IV, Beverly (Lambert) Bush, Louise (Mucken) Manegre, Margaret (Jensen) Reichenback, Hazel (Kirk) Blackerby, Agnes (McKay) Hemshorn, Sr. Marian Theresa, S.N.J.M. (Louise Mullen), Rowena (Warren) Murphy, Charles "Pling" Pelland, Florence (Ray) Lull, Dolores "Ducky" (Raymond) Bustamonte and Leo Smith.

My daughter, Suzanne McKay, spent many hours editing the material, and I am sure that her work adds to the book's readability.

My brother, Joseph McKay, spent many hours visiting the various families with me, and in general, contributed to the project in many ways, such as researching special items and collecting pictures.

Elizabeth (McKay) Allured, my daughter, did extensive research on subjects that had to be clarified if the real story were to be told.

My daughter, Diane McKay, assisted with the editing, furnished art work and photos and "fine tuned" the text.

For two years in the 1930's, while attending the University of Portland, I lived with my great-aunt, Mary McKay, who was born in St. Paul in 1851 and lived there until 1900. I am greatly indebted to her for the education about St. Paul that she provided and for the written records which she maintained.

I would like to thank my long-time friend, Edward O'Meara, managing editor of the *Oregon Journal*, for his guidance and counseling; the St. Paul Mission Historical Society for the use of their facilities when I was finalizing the project; and my wife, Genevieve, for typing the final draft of the manuscript.

Many others contributed and I express my appreciation to each person who participated.

This book is certainly not a complete history of everything that happened in the St. Paul area, but it does represent a base upon which others may wish to build.

H.J.M.

CONTENTS

Part Three — Individuals In Their Own Words

THE ST. PAUL AREA

Up until about 1850, the small communities in the Willamette Valley were known as settlements. Some of these early settlements were Oregon City, Canemah (just above the Oregon City falls), La Butte (Butteville), Champoeg, the St. Paul Catholic Mission (St. Paul), the Methodist Mission, Chemeketa (Salem), Dayton, Yamhill Falls (Lafayette) and Grand Prairie (St. Louis).

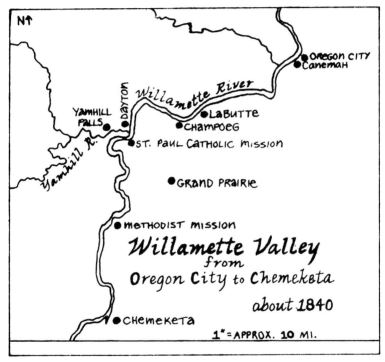

The St. Paul Catholic Mission was located about one mile northwest of the Willamette River and about one mile and a half north-northwest of the spot where the Yamhill River empties into the Willamette. The settlements which were nearest to St. Paul were Champoeg, which was about five miles north; Dayton, which was about four miles northwest and across the river; and St. Louis, which was about six miles to the southeast.

In 1826, the Hudson's Bay Company established what was perhaps the first ferry across the Willamette River.

The ferry ran from a point about two miles northwest of present-day St. Paul to a point directly across the river about one mile below where the Yamhill River empties into the Willamette near Dayton. The Indians had used the same crossing point because the river was narrow there during the summertime and there was a wide gravel beach. About 1840, a Mr. Jean Baptiste Deguire apparently purchased the ferry operation and took up a land claim that included the site where the ferry and landing were located. The property then became known as Deguire's Ferry and Landing. This ferry made travel between the St. Paul area and Yamhill County relatively easy.

In this book, when used to show the location of land claims, landings and other settlements, the term "St. Paul" means the city limits of present-day St. Paul, Oregon. The term "St. Paul area" means an area within a radius of approximately three and one-half miles of the city limits of present-day St. Paul, Oregon.

This book is based on information obtained from books and articles on the early history of the Pacific Northwest and on information contained in the personal records of thirty-two families whose ancestors came to St. Paul between 1820 and 1890. A synopsis of each of these families comprises Part Two. It is much easier to understand the story of St. Paul when the background, character and personality of the people who lived there are known. Conversly, it would be difficult to understand each family story without knowing the story of St. Paul itself. Obviously there were more than thirty-two families who settled in the St. Paul area during the 1820-1890 period, and there was no intent to limit this book to thirty-two families. In many cases, in the time available, it was not possible to locate a descendant of some of the early families who were known to have lived there. The thirty-two families included are perhaps typical of all the families who lived in the St. Paul area during the 1820-1890 period.

PART I

A HISTORY OF EVENTS IN THE ST. PAUL AREA

CHAPTER 1

THE EXPLORERS AND FUR TRAPPERS

The region known as the Oregon Country was the northern half of the area between the Rocky Mountains and the Pacific Ocean. The northern and northwestern boundaries were roughly the Arctic Circle and the present day Alaskan-Russian border. The southern boundary was roughly a line running from the Rocky Mountains to the Pacific Ocean connecting with and paralleling the present day Oregon-California border.

The Oregon Country was inhabited by Indians. The early explorers found that the Chinook Indians lived along both sides of the Columbia River from Celilo Falls to the Pacific Ocean. They also lived on both sides of the Willamette above the Willamette River falls. The Chinooks were friendly Indians and were expert fishermen. Their leader was Chief Concomly. When Lewis and Clark returned east in 1806 they gave their stockade and crude huts to Coboway, the chief of the Clatsop tribe. The Clatsops were one of the tribes of the Chinook Nation. The Calapooian Indians lived along the Willamette above the Willamette River falls. They were also friendly but their manner of living was not as highly developed as that of the Chinooks. In the early 1800's, both the Chinook and Calapooian Indians had suffered great loss of life due to the introduction of white people's diseases to which they had very little resistance.

In the early 1800's the Astor Party of 1810-1812 and their Pacific Fur Company, the Northwest Fur Company from Montreal, Canada, and a few scattered individuals were ex-

The Willamette River one mile northwest of St. Paul

Trap used by an early day fur trapper in the St. Paul area

ploring and trapping in the Columbia and Willamette River Valleys. As the early explorers and trappers left the Columbia and entered the Willamette River in their canoes, they navigated through thick forests of tall trees for about thirty miles. Then, at a place the Indians called Champoeg, they found a small prairie, an area of land where no timber was growing, fronting the river. Its highest point was about 40 feet above the river. In exploring the area further they found that there were additional larger prairies to the south and southwest, which did not extend to the river's bank, and which were less likely to be flooded in times of high water. These larger prairies were near present day St. Paul, Oregon. As they explored further they found that there were additional large prairies south, southeast and east of the St. Paul area. They also found that there was an abundance of game in the Willamette River Valley. Because of the abundance of fur producing animals, the Northwest Fur Company established the Willamette Trading Post in 1813, about three miles west of Champoeg and about three miles north of St. Paul.

As fur trapping developed in the Willamette Valley, the trappers began to assemble each spring, prior to the annual expedition, on the Champoeg-St. Paul prairies. After about six months they would return with their furs to this same area. Some of the men who had previously been fur trappers in Canada and the Rocky Mountain area had Indian wives. Most of the other trappers eventually married Indian or part-Indian women. Each year the entire families, including the children, would make the treck. With each passing year the expedition would go farther south as the amount of game in the areas near their rendezvous point decreased. Eventually they went as far south as present day California. Most of the trappers were French Canadian. Many of them stayed on the Champoeg-St. Paul prairies during the winter, and some of them eventually settled there. The trappers later settled on the prairies south, southeast and east of present day St. Paul. This prairie complex became known as French Prairie because so many French Canadians lived there.

By 1814, the Northwest Fur Company almost completely controlled the fur trading industry in the Willamette Valley, as the Pacific Fur Company had discontinued operations the previous year. In 1821 the Northwest Fur Company became part of the larger Hudson's Bay Company, which had been conducting fur trading in Canada.

In 1826, the Hudson's Bay Company established perhaps the first ferry across the Willamette River. The ferry ran from a point about two miles northwest of present day St. Paul to a point directly across the river, about one mile below where the Yamhill River empties into the Willamette near present day Dayton. The Indians had used the same crossing point because the river was narrow there and there was a wide gravel beach. This ferry and landing site was probably a factor when a site for the Catholic Mission was chosen—a decision which established the location of present day St. Paul.

Fir trees with Willamette River in the background. Some of the fir trees were more than five feet in diameter and more than two hundred feet high.

CHAPTER 2

THE HUDSON'S BAY COMPANY AND FRENCH CANADIAN FARMS

By 1829, some of the men who were married and had families wanted to obtain land for farming. This, however, was against the policy of the Hudson's Bay Company, which was virtually the only source of agricultural seeds. The company, being English, operated in accordance with Great Britain's territorial interests and goals.

Dr. John McLoughlin was the manager of the Oregon Country operations for the Hudson's Bay Company. His headquarters was at Fort Vancouver. He was later to become known as "Father of the Oregon Country".

In 1829, Dr. McLoughlin convinced the company headquarters in London that the agricultural seed policy should be slightly relaxed. As a result he was able to give agricultural seeds to three men who had come with the Astor Party —two French Canadians and an Englishman. Each of these men had married a daughter of Coboway, a chief of the Clatsop Indian tribe living just south of the Columbia River where it enters the Pacific Ocean. The two French Canadians chose farming sites on French Prairie and were followed each year thereafter by additional ex-fur trappers who likewise started farms. By 1838, there were 26 farms in the area, and most of them were operated by French Canadians with Indian wives. By that time the four most prominent French Canadian settlers were Etienne Lucier, Joseph Gervais, Louis Labonte and Pierre Belleque. Lucier, Gervais and Labonte had arrived with the Astor Party in 1811-1812 and Belleque had come with the Northwest Fur Company in 1818. Joseph Gervais married Yaimust of the Clatsop Indian tribe and Louis Labonte married her sister, Kilakotah. Yaimust and Kilakotah were daughters of Coboway, Chief of the Clatsop Indian tribe. As a young girl Kilakotah, the chief's eldest daughter, had probably seen Lewis and Clark. Etienne Lucier married Josephite of the Nouete Indian tribe. Pierre Belleque married Genevieve

Dr. John McLoughlin

Clackamas County Historical Society

A wheat field at harvest time

St. Martin, daughter of Joseph St. Martin, an early fur
trapper, and a Chinook Indian woman.

One of the earliest places where the French Canadians
settled or started farms was an area within a radius of about
three and a half miles of present day St. Paul. This area
contained prairies, a ferry across the river, a small Catholic
log church, and a flour mill and saw mill which the Hudson's Bay Company had constructed about three miles east
of St. Paul on Champoeg Creek.

Two of the earliest settlers in this area were the previously
mentioned Pierre Belleque and Etienne Lucier. Belleque's
farm was three miles north of St. Paul. The old Willamette
Trading Post building was on his land. Lucier's farm was
about three and a half miles north of St. Paul and just west
of Belleque's farm. Both farms were started about 1830 and
were quite large.

Jacques Servant, a native of Montreal, who came west
about 1812-1815, married Josephite of the Okanagan Indian tribe in the early 1820's and had a farm one mile south-
southeast of St. Paul by the late 1830's. Augustin Raymond,
a native of Montreal, who came west in the early 1830's, had
a farm about a mile and a half south-southeast of St. Paul by
about 1835 and married Jacques Servant's daughter Marie
in 1843. Louis Bergevin, a Canadian native, came west in
the early 1840's and had a farm two miles south of St. Paul
by the middle 1840's. He married Jacques Servant's
daughter Madeline shortly after her first husband, Charles
Jeaudoin, died in 1848.

Louis Pichet, an early fur trapper from Montreal, came
west about 1820 and later was a courier for the Hudson's
Bay Company. He married Marguerite Bercier and settled
on a farm about two and a half miles southeast of St. Paul
by the late 1830's. Marguerite Bercier was the daughter of
Antoine Bercier, who had come west about 1810 with the
Northwest Fur Company, and Emelie Fenlay, whose father, Francois Fenlay, had been an early fur trapper in the
Northern Rocky Mountain area and had married Giget of
the Cree Indian Nation some time prior to 1795.

Jean Baptiste Deguire, an early fur trapper in the Rocky
Mountains, came to St. Paul in 1840. His wife, Mary Anne

Perrault, was the daughter of another early fur trapper, Jean Perrault, and a Chinook Indian woman. Mr. Deguire had a farm and ferry operation about two miles northwest of St. Paul by the early 1840's.

David Mongrain, a native of Canada, came west with the Hudson's Bay Company in 1830 and had a farm two and a half miles southeast of St. Paul by about 1840. He married Catherine Lafantaisie, daughter of Jacques Lafantaisie, who came to Astoria on the ill-fated TONQUIN in 1811.

Thomas Liard, another native of Canada, came west in the early 1840's and had a farm two miles east of St. Paul by about 1846. His wife, Celeste Rocbrune, was the daughter of Joseph Rocbrune, a native of Montreal who came west in the late 1820's with the Hudson's Bay Company and married Lisette of the Walla Walla Indian tribe some time in the early 1830's.

Francois Bernier, a native of Maskinonge, Canada, came to St. Paul in the early 1840's. He worked as a miller and had a farm about two miles south-southeast of St. Paul shortly after arriving. He married Etienne Lucier's daughter Pelagie in 1843.

Many other individuals, who had been independent fur trappers or had been employed by fur trading companies, lived in the St. Paul area, which is only a small part of French Prairie, during the 1820-1842 period.

The previously mentioned twenty-six families who lived on French Prairie in 1838 had increased to eighty-three by 1842. The fact that this group of mostly French Canadian-Indian families existed in the Willamette Valley was a considerable factor in maintaining peaceful relations between the Canadian and American immigrants and the various Indian nations in the Oregon Country during the 1815-1847 period.

The families raised wheat, oats, legumes, vegetables and fruit on their farms. They had horses, cattle, swine and sheep. In addition to farming, hewing logs was a rather extensive activity, since most of the homes and other buildings were constructed from logs. Stories handed down indicate that a Mr. Laderoute was the best log beam hewer on French Prairie. Their steadily increasing farm produce was sold to the Hudson's Bay Company. The farmers would take the produce to a river landing to be loaded on a canoe, keelboat or flatboat powered by Indian oarsmen for the trip to Champoeg, Oregon City or Fort Vancouver. In some cases the produce was taken by wagon to Champoeg, where the Hudson's Bay Company established a warehouse in 1841. Produce with a destination north of Champoeg would be unloaded at Canemah, just above the Oregon City falls, and portaged around the falls to Oregon City, where it would be retained for use or shipped to Fort Vancouver. Each Indian oarsman received $16 for the round trip from the various French Prairie landings to Canemah.

In 1841, Duflot de Mofras, a representative of the French government, visited the Oregon Country. In his official report on his return to France, he stated that 30,000 bushels of wheat and 10,000 bushels of other grains were stored in the Hudson's Bay Company warehouse at Champoeg in the fall of 1841. He also reported that the settlers were eager to obtain information about friends and relatives, and in general to find out how everything was in France.

Most of the French Canadians were Catholics, but there were no priests or Catholic churches in the area. Therefore, during the 1831-1835 period the French Canadians petitioned the Catholic Church for priests. At the suggestion of Dr. John McLoughlin, petitions were sent to Monsignor Provencher in Red River, Winnipeg, Canada, on July 3, 1834, and again on February 23, 1835. The Hudson's Bay Company had originally opposed this but Dr. McLoughlin had persuaded them to relent. The farmers and Indians started to build a church on French Prairie. The log church was completed in 1836, but three years were to pass before the arrival of a priest.

Father (later Archbishop) Francois Blanchet

Archives, Archdiocese of Portland in Oregon

Replica of log church constructed in 1836

The Oregonian

CHAPTER 3

A MISSION IN THE WILDERNESS

In response to the requests for priests, the Bishop of Quebec, Bishop Joseph Signay, appointed Father Francois Norbert Blanchet as the Vicar General for the Oregon Country Missions. Father Blanchet and Father Modeste Demers, Father Blanchet's assistant, arrived at Fort Vancouver from Montreal with a Hudson's Bay Company group on November 24, 1838. Because it was the policy of the Hudson's Bay Company that priests could not reside south of the Columbia River, Father Blanchet planned to go as a visitor to the church on French Prairie, where the settlers and Indians were waiting for him. In early January, after the people on French Prairie had been advised that Father Blanchet would be arriving at the church, Etienne Lucier and Pierre Belleque from French Prairie went to Fort Vancouver to meet Father Blanchet and accompany him to French Prairie. They arrived back at the church on January 5, 1839.

On January 6, the Feast of the Epiphany, Father Blanchet blessed the French Prairie church and celebrated the first Mass south of the Columbia River in the Oregon Country. He dedicated the church, which was located in the midst of the farms, to the Apostle Paul. He then set about baptizing and marrying the settlers and their wives and baptizing their children. Almost all of the French Canadian-Indian families in the area were there. The day was unusually warm for that time of year, which the Indians considered a good omen. A new dimension had been added to the lives of the people in the St. Paul area.

On October 9, 1839, Father Blanchet received a letter from Governor James Douglas of the Hudson's Bay Company which changed the previous residence policy and allowed priests to reside south of the Columbia River. Father Blanchet then selected a 2,500 acre tract of land for a Catholic mission. The log church was on the land claim. In addition to providing for normal church activities, Father Blanchet hired farmers to cultivate the land,

and supervised the construction of schools for children and apprentice shops for adults.

On September 17, 1842, Father Langlois and Father Bolduc arrived in St. Paul from Canada. They began work on St. Joseph's College, which was to be a boys' school at the mission. The college opened in 1843 with 30 students in attendance. Later, a Mr. Joseph Larocque of Paris was to donate 4,000 francs for the school. Father Langlois was placed in charge of St. Joseph's College.

The previously mentioned Duflot de Mofras noted in his official report to the French government that about 600 French Canadians attended Mass at the St. Paul Catholic Church when he was there in 1841, and that the church was located on a farm containing about 2,500 acres.

In 1842, Father Pierre DeSmet, a Jesuit priest who had missions among the Flathead Indians, arrived in St. Paul seeking help for his missions. After a discussion with Father Blanchet, who was also seeking help, Father DeSmet decided to go to Europe and see if he could obtain missionaries there.

On August 17, 1844, Father DeSmet, who was by that time in charge of all Catholic missions in the Oregon Country, arrived back in St. Paul from Europe. "The Padre of the Mountains", as he was known, brought with him four priests, a number of lay brothers and six Sisters of Notre Dame de Namur. He took up a land claim about a mile west of St. Paul and on it established St. Francis Xavier Mission.

Father DeSmet and his contingent, with the aid of French Canadians and Indians, cleared away brush and erected a 45 feet by 35 feet two-story log house, three shops and several barns. One of the priests was a medical doctor, so he treated the settlers and the Indians in the surrounding area. At the time a disease known as "bloody flux" had struck almost everybody in the area.

The large two-story house was Father DeSmet's dream of a motherhouse for the use of the mountain missions that he had or would later establish. It was to be a place where the missionaries would study Indian languages, make retreats and rest. He envisioned that eventually it would be a novitiate where Americans would be trained by experienced

Left: Father (later Bishop) Modeste Demers   Right: Father Pierre DeSmet

Archives, Archdiocese of Portland in Oregon

Jesuits to be missionaries. It was also to be a central Jesuit supply center. However, even though it had beauty and charm, the St. Francis Xavier Mission simply could not be an efficient headquarters for missions which were as far as 500 hazardous miles away. In addition, it was 55 miles from Fort Vancouver, a distance which took two days and cost $16 to traverse. But for a while—about five years—St. Francis Xavier Mission, the Jesuit headquarters for the Oregon Country missions, existed and performed commendably for all of the Catholic missions in the 375,000 square mile Oregon Country.

The six Sisters of Notre Dame de Namur, who came from Europe with Father DeSmet via Cape Horn on the chartered ship INDEFATIGABLE, arrived at St. Paul on August 17, 1844. On September 9, the Sisters opened a school for women and girls in St. Paul. The academy, the first in Oregon, was not completed until October; so their first lessons were given outdoors. There were thirty pupils the first year, ranging in age from 16 to 60. They camped in the woods and prepared for their First Communion while attending school. They paid for their education with flour, meat, eggs, salt, candles and tea. Most of the students were members of the French Canadian-Indian families. The Sisters opened a second school at Oregon City in 1848.

In November 1844, Father Blanchet received word that he had been nominated to be bishop. The next month he left for Europe to be consecrated. After arriving there he found that he would have to go to Montreal, where he was

St. Paul Catholic Church—1846

known, to be consecrated. He then sailed from England to Montreal, where he was consecrated on July 25, 1845. He returned to Europe to see if he could obtain additional priests and money. He visited Rome and other main cities, meeting with two different popes and many other dignitaries. He was able to arrange for missionaries and was given financial assistance. Furthermore, on July 24, 1846, he was appointed archbishop. He returned to the St. Paul Mission in August 1847.

On May 24, 1846, the cornerstone was laid and construction begun on a new brick church at St. Paul. The project was under the direction of Father Demers, who was acting Vicar General in the absence of Bishop Blanchet. The church was completed on November 1, 1846. It contained 160,000 bricks and cost $20,000 to build. It was 100 feet long, 45 feet wide, had two 15 feet by 15 feet side chapels and an 84 feet high belfry, and was cruciform in shape. Its bell tolled three times each day, and on occasions of special joy or when a parishioner died. The new church was a very distinctive landmark for St. Paul.

When Archbishop Blanchet returned from Europe on August 19, 1847, he brought twenty-two new workers with him. On September 12, he administered the Sacrament of Confirmation at St. Paul. He ordained the first priest, Father J. F. Jayol, on September 19, and the second priest, Father Bartholemew DeLorme, on October 31, in the St. Paul church. These men were the first priests ordained in the Oregon Country.

November 30, 1847 was an eventful day in the history of St. Paul, for on that day Father Modeste Demers, who had come to the Oregon Country with the then Father Blanchet eight years earlier, and who had learned the Indian language and built the new brick church, was consecrated bishop in the new church. He was appointed Bishop of Vancouver Island. He was the first bishop to be consecrated in the Oregon Country; and everybody from the youngest to the oldest, including the new American immigrants, came to the ceremony. They came in wagons and carts, on horseback and on foot, for this momentous occasion.

The St. Paul Catholic Mission—1847

St. Paul Mission Historical Society

CHAPTER 4

THE ESTABLISHMENT OF
A PROVISIONAL GOVERNMENT IN 1843

Until about 1840, only a handful of Americans had come to the Oregon Country. A few more came in small groups in 1840 and 1841. In 1842, the first organized wagon train crossed the plains from Missouri to the Willamette Valley. The group consisted of about 125 people led by Dr. Elijah White. After arriving, about half of them decided to continue south to California, which was then part of Mexico.

The Americans in the Willamette Valley were interested in taking action which would eventually result in the Oregon Country being part of the United States. There was no organized government at the time. The Americans believed that some sort of government was needed for organized protection against the wild animals, especially the wolves; and for purposes of issuing titles to land, settling disputes and, in general, maintaining law and order among a population which was obviously going to increase quite rapidly.

This desire for an organized government created quite a problem for Dr. McLoughlin and the Hudson's Bay Company, which had controlled so many things until that time. The Hudson's Bay Company had achieved its dominant position while the United States-Great Britain joint occupancy agreement was in effect, and the loyalty of the Hudson's Bay Company was to Great Britain.

After a series of "Wolf Meetings", one of which was held at the St. Paul Mission, a meeting was scheduled to be held at Champoeg on May 2, 1843, for the purpose of determining whether or not a majority desired an organized government.

On May 2 at Champoeg, a government was approved by a 52 to 50 vote. All of the Americans and a few of the French Canadians voted for the government. This was the first provisional government established west of the Rocky Mountains.

Champoeg Meeting—May 2, 1843

The Provisional Government brought about major changes and greatly reduced the power of the Hudson's Bay Company. The situation remained joint occupancy until 1846; but from May 2, 1843 until Oregon became a territory in 1848, the government was to be controlled by the Americans.

Champoeg was the first capital of the Provisional Government, but its status lasted for only a little more than a year. Oregon City was designated as the capital in 1844. The Provisional Government brought about better organization, and as a result individual and property rights were more formally defined and protection against wild animals was improved. The process did not occur overnight but came about gradually as government statutes were refined to meet requirements of the time.

In 1843, Champoeg was the center of commercial activity for French Prairie. In 1844, a passenger boat line, propelled by Indian paddlers, was established between Champoeg and Canemah. It left Champoeg on Mondays and Thursdays, and Canemah on Wednesdays and Saturdays.

The French Canadians continued to operate and expand their farms. By 1843, they had approximately 3,000 cattle, 1,800 horses, 500 sheep and 3,000 swine, and were producing about 150,000 bushels of wheat annually. Most of the wheat was harvested by flailing, but some was harvested by small harvesters which were made in local blacksmith shops. The surplus produce was taken to Champoeg by wagon or riverboat. The two earliest landings near St. Paul were the previously mentioned Deguire's Landing and Mission Landing, which was located about a mile west-northwest of St. Paul about a mile above where the Yamhill empties into the Willamette. After the grain and other produce arrived in Champoeg most of it was shipped to Canemah for further shipment to Oregon City and Fort Vancouver.

Immigrants continued to arrive in the Oregon Country in ever increasing numbers. About 800 people arrived in the Willamette Valley in 1843. An additional 1,400 came in 1844 and another 3,000 came in 1845. Some went on to California. One of the 1844 immigrants to the Willamette Valley who went to California, James Marshall, was to be the first person to discover gold there. Peter Burnett, who came in 1843 and became Chief Justice of the Supreme Court for the Provisional Government, later went south to California and became the first American governor of that state. John Sutter arrived in Oregon by ship from the Sandwich Islands (Hawaiian Islands), and later went to California and established Sutter's Fort near Sacramento. But most of the early immigrants who came to the Willamette Valley settled there.

In 1846, after many disagreements with the Hudson's Bay Company, the 6 feet 7 inch Dr. John McLoughlin, who was also known as "Father of the Oregon Country" and "The White-Headed Eagle", resigned as the Oregon Country Manager for the company. He had become controversial because he had tried to please both sides, which had been competing for control of the area. Considering the position he was in, one can see that his accomplishments were outstanding. During the twenty-one years when he had been at the helm of the Hudson's Bay Company in the Oregon Country, there had been relatively peaceful relations with the Indians and an organized government had been established for the area.

In March of 1846, under contract with the Provisional Government, Hugh Burns carried the first mail across the plains. He rode alone by horseback, taking six months for the round trip from Oregon City to Weston, Missouri. He had come to Oregon in 1842 and had been elected one of the three magistrates when the Provisional Government was established at Champoeg. Many of his relatives were to be among the early American immigrants who were to settle among the French Canadian-Indian families in the St. Paul area.

A few families living in the St. Paul area were British Canadian-Indian, but St. Paul was still a basically French Canadian-Indian settlement composed mainly of farm families in 1846. These farmers continued to produce basic items such as wheat, oats, potatoes, vegetables, meat and fruit. Many children were attending the mission schools. There were plenty of wild animals in the area, so game was abundant. The large mission was an integral part of the community, and because it was the headquarters for the Catholic Church in the Oregon Country it had greater status than an average mission. People were relatively happy, but with the ever increasing number of immigrants coming to the Willamette Valley it was obvious that changes were inevitable. Their new brick church was an example of changes that could occur. They must have been proud of their accomplishments, and undoubtedly were looking to the future with a feeling of great optimism.

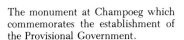

The monument at Champoeg which commemorates the establishment of the Provisional Government.

Champoeg State Park Collection

CHAPTER 5

THE IMMIGRATION OF 1847

The trend of yearly increases in the number of American immigrants continued in 1847. This was the year that the immigrants carried measles. Not only did they have measles themselves, but as they passed through the various Indian settlements they left measles and death in their wake.

After they passed through the Cayuse Indian country, many Indians came down with measles and died. The Indians thought that Dr. Marcus Whitman, the Methodist missionary in their area, had poisoned them and they became very upset. The Whitman Massacre followed on November 29, 1847. The relatively peaceful relationship that had existed between the Indians and the immigrants in the Oregon Country until that time deteriorated rapidly.

As the 1847 immigrants passed through present day Portland they saw only one brick building, two white houses and a few log cabins. Oregon City and Canemah, with warehouses, blacksmith shops, sawmills, plough and wagon factories, flour mills, small stores and hotels, were developed to a much greater extent.

Two Irish-American immigrants had settled in St. Paul in 1846. They were Miles McDonald, 20, a native of Armagh, County Armagh, Ireland, who had come to Oregon via Cape Horn on a steamship; and John Cooke, 18, a native of County Limerick, Ireland, who had crossed the plains with the Applegate wagon train. They helped build the new brick church after they arrived.

A small number of the 1847 immigrants settled in the St. Paul area. They were perhaps the first American immigrant families to settle there. Previously the settlement had consisted of the Catholic missionaries, the French Canadians and their Indian or part-Indian wives, and a few single Americans such as McDonald and Cooke.

The American immigrant families who came to St. Paul in 1847 were the Hugh Cosgroves, the James McKays, the John and Barney Kennedys, and the James Colemans. The Cosgroves and McKays came together in a thirteen-family wagon train under the leadership of Lot Whitcomb of later Oregon steamboat fame. According to stories handed down through the Kennedy family, the Kennedy families came with this same group. The Colemans came with a party under the leadership of Captain Davidson and Captain Mendenhall.

Hugh Cosgrove, 45, was a native of County Cavan, Northern Ireland. His wife, Mary (Rositer) Cosgrove, about 36, was a native of Perth, Canada, where they had been married in 1825. They had six daughters and two sons. The Cosgroves had conducted several successful business ventures in Michigan and Illinois and were relatively wealthy by the standards of the time.

James McKay, 29, was a native of Belfast, Northern Ireland; and Cecelia (Lawson) McKay, 25, was a native of Dundee, Scotland, where they had been married in 1840. Mr. McKay was a Catholic and Mrs. McKay was a Presbyterian. As both of their families were against the marriage because of the religious difference, they had eloped and come to the United States. When they left Joliet, Illinois,they had two small sons, but both died from measles during the journey near The Dalles, Oregon.

The Kennedy families were in their early thirties and were natives of County Donegal, Ireland. They had come from Louisa County, Iowa, but had previously lived in Joliet, Illinois. Mr. and Mrs. Barney Kennedy had a two-year old son; and John Kennedy, whose wife had died, had a five-year old daughter.

James Coleman, 26, of Dutch descent, was born in Pennsylvania; and Frances (Murray) Coleman, 23, was a native of Ireland. They were married in 1845 in Louisa County, Iowa, and had a year-old daughter who accompanied them across the plains.

After arriving in St. Paul, Hugh Cosgrove purchased a 320 acre farm from a French Canadian for $800, two oxen and two cows. The land was adjacent to the mission and extended about a mile to the east. It included a fairly good house. Mr. Cosgrove planted 40 acres of wheat during the fall.

John and Barney Kennedy each took up a land claim about three and one-half miles east of St. Paul. Barney Kennedy's place, which was purchased from a Mr. Doughrain, contained a small round log cabin.

After James McKay arrived in St. Paul, he purchased the old mission mill property from Archbishop Blanchet for $8,000 on January 28, 1848. He did not have the money but agreed to pay with earnings from the flour mill and sawmill. He also took up a 640 acre land claim adjacent to the mill property so that he would have logs for the sawmill. The mills were about three miles east of St. Paul on Champoeg Creek. They had been constructed by the Hudson's Bay Company and had been sold to Archbishop Blanchet in 1845.

James McKay, Miles McDonald and James Coleman operated the Mission Mills during the fall and winter of 1847-1848. John Cooke stayed at the St. Paul Mission and worked for Archbishop Blanchet. The Cosgroves and Kennedys spent their time on their farms.

The fall and winter of 1847-48 was an interesting time for the newly arrived American immigrants in the St. Paul area. They were getting settled in their new community where tall fir trees, scattered prairies, the Willamette River, French Canadian-Indian families, log houses and a large mission were the dominant characteristics. The prairies were surrounded by heavily timbered areas; and, especially along the creeks, many of the fir trees were 200 feet tall and four to five feet in diameter at the base. The settlers were busy clearing small patches of land and building small houses for those who did not have a house on their claim, and building small sheds for their animals. For most, their social life centered around the mission, where each Sunday they would visit with each other, their French Canadian neighbors, the priests and sisters. After Mass they would return to their homes by horseback or in their wagons.

In late fall of 1847, word was received that a party had been sent to obtain the release of the Americans being held hostage by the Indians after the Whitman Massacre. There were rumors that there might be a war with the Cayuse Indians and that an Oregon Army might be organized.

Covered wagon

Oregon Historical Society

Oregon City in 1847

Clackamas County Historical Society

Shortly thereafter an Oregon Volunteer Army was organized and John Cooke, Narcisse Cornoyer and other French Canadians joined and left for eastern Oregon.

Augustin Lambert and Catherine (Pichet) Lambert, both natives of Montreal, and their six-year-old son, Augustin II, arrived in St. Paul in late 1847. Augustin I had previously been in Oregon from about 1840 until 1846, when he returned to Canada to get his wife and young son. After arriving the Lamberts lived in a log cabin which Mr. Lambert had built on their land claim, about eight miles southeast of St. Paul. They were later to move to the St. Paul area and conduct extensive logging operations for many years.

Many American immigrants were settling across the Willamette River in Yamhill County. The largest settlements there were Yamhill Falls and Dayton. In 1847, the name of Yamhill Falls was changed to Lafayette, and a city was platted there. Both Dayton and Lafayette were on the Yamhill River, which emptied into the Willamette almost directly across from St. Paul. After visiting in Yamhill County, James Coleman and Miles McDonald took up donation land claims there. However, they did not move to their claims until 1848.

In order to better organize the operations of the Catholic Church in the Pacific Northwest, Archbishop Blanchet called the First Provisional Council. It was to be held in St. Paul and would be attended by Archbishop Blanchet, Vicar General for the Oregon Country, Bishop Modeste Demers of Fort Vancouver and Bishop Maglorie Blanchet of Walla Walla. The First Provisional Council was held in St. Paul on February 28, 1848.

By the spring of 1848, the new American immigrant families could look with satisfaction on their venture. They had been able to obtain the necessary food and supplies from their French Canadian neighbors. They had come through their first winter in good shape, and the winter rains were gradually diminishing. They were becoming settled and were able to enjoy the feeling of stability after the long journey which had started a year earlier.

With the coming of spring the James Colemans and Miles McDonald took the ferry to Yamhill County, and settled on their land claims there.

In early May, a veritable bolt of lightning from the south struck French Prairie. It was to change drastically the plans of almost everybody in the Willamette Valley.

The church bell was cast in Belgium in 1845 and installed in the church tower in 1846. Since that time the sounds from this five hundred pound bell have been a distinctive part of the St. Paul environment.

St. Paul Mission Historical Society Collection

CHAPTER 6

THE GOLD RUSH

On January 24, 1848, James Marshall—who, as mentioned earlier, had come to the Willamette Valley in 1844 before going to California—discovered gold in the American River near Sacramento. At first the discovery was not publicized very much because nobody knew how much gold there was. But as more people prospected they found that gold could be found all over the area.

The first people outside of California to receive word of the discovery were the people in the Willamette Valley and the Mormons in Utah. They were not only the closest to the discovery, but, especially in the case of the people in the Willamette Valley, were friends with many of the people in the Sacramento area as they had come across the plains with them. These friends and acquaintances passed the word.

Rumors of the discovery of gold were received in St. Paul in the spring of 1848 and were verified shortly thereafter. Obviously the discovery presented a once-in-a-lifetime

Gold mining

opportunity. Almost immediately practically everybody in the area decided to go to the gold fields. Eventually two out of every three able-bodied men and a few women hurried to the gold fields in the summer and fall of 1848 or in early 1849.

A St. Paul contingent, including French Canadians and some of the 1847 immigrants, decided to leave in early summer of 1848. They made the necessary repairs to their wagons and packed the necessary provisions. They arranged for the operation of their farms and the flour mills during their absence. The group included some French Canadians, Hugh Cosgrove, John Kennedy and Mr. and Mrs. James McKay. Barney Kennedy stayed home to operate both Kennedy farms. Before leaving, Mrs. McKay was baptized as a Catholic, with Archbishop Blanchet as her godfather and Mrs. Cosgrove as her godmother. It was not long after the group left that many French Canadian-Indians started to contract cholera. Many of them died or returned to St. Paul before reaching their goal, and those who returned brought cholera back with them. Since the part-Indian families had very little resistance to this white people's disease, it was especially disastrous to them.

Because so many people were leaving the Willamette Valley to go to the gold fields, St. Joseph's College was closed and the operation of the Sisters of Notre Dame School was greatly curtailed. The farms and mills were being run by the elderly men, young boys and women who remained in St. Paul.

At this time there was much unrest among the Indians. Some Indians, who were tried for their part in the Whitman Massacre, were hanged in Oregon City, which by then was the capital for the Provisional Government. As a result of this unrest among the Indians, women and children hid in their homes at night. The number of people attending the St. Paul church decreased dramatically and for a time the Provisional Government suspended missionary activity in the Oregon Country. The settlements which had been developing so rapidly and so well were having real problems.

When the St. Paul group arrived in the Sacramento area, they found, in addition to cholera and yellow fever, "gold dust fever", a rather severe respiratory ailment. Hugh Cosgrove and John Kennedy mined for gold and made a considerable amount of money. The McKays opened a combination tavern and store and made in excess of $10,000. In addition, Mrs. McKay wrote letters for illiterate miners, a service for which she received gold dust or gold nuggets. Hugh Cosgrove, John Kennedy and Mr. and Mrs. McKay arrived back in St. Paul in December 1848 after a very successful "spur of the moment" adventure.

James McKay paid Archbishop Blanchet the $8,000 he had agreed to pay for the mill property, and had money left over. He set about repairing and improving the mills. There was a great demand for flour and lumber at inflated prices generated by the gold rush. Hugh Cosgrove put his six daughters in the Sisters of Notre Dame School at Oregon City and prepared to return to the gold fields early the next year with his wife and two sons. The Kennedys decided that Barney Kennedy would go to the gold fields early in 1849 and that this time John Kennedy would run their farms. It was a time of much activity in St. Paul.

The news of the California gold discovery reached St. Louis, Missouri in the fall of 1848. Almost immediately nearly all who were able to finance the trip, and some who weren't, were either leaving immediately or planning to leave in the spring of 1849. People who had been planning on coming to Oregon via the Oregon Trail changed their plans and decided to take the more hazardous southern route over the Sierra Nevadas and go directly to California. This reduced the immigration to Oregon to a trickle in 1849. Not only was the Oregon Country losing people to California, which had become a United States Territory in the spring of 1848, but virtually no new people were coming to Oregon.

After the discovery of gold, people began to hear of the large amounts some prospectors were finding. The desire to be in on the opportunity spurred a number of Catholics from St. Paul, Champoeg, Oregon City, St. Louis and Fort Vancouver to set off for the gold fields in 1849. With the consent of Archbishop Blanchet, Father DeLorme accompanied them as their spiritual advisor. Among the St. Paul residents who left in early 1849, probably with the Catholic Brigade, were Pierre Belleque and his 13-year old son, Pierre II; Francois Bernier; Augustin Raymond; Louis Labonte II; Barney Kennedy; James Coleman, who left his wife and small daughter at the mission during his absence from his Yamhill County farm; Mr. and Mrs. Cosgrove and their two small sons, one of whom was an infant; and Father DeLorme. The Belleques, Bernier, Labonte II, Raymond, Coleman and Kennedy were very successful prospectors. The Cosgroves opened a store for miners near Sacramento. In October 1849, Pierre Belleque and his son and Father DeLorme left San Francisco for St. Paul by steamship. On the way home tragedy struck when the elder Belleque and Father DeLorme contracted yellow fever. Belleque died and was buried at sea but Father Delorme survived. On October 21, Father DeLorme and young Pierre Belleque returned to St. Paul. Francois Bernier, Louis Labonte II, Augustin Raymond, James Coleman and Barney Kennedy returned to St. Paul in December 1849 after a very successful adventure.

Oregon became a United States Territory on August 13, 1848. The news did not reach Oregon until Territorial Governor Lane arrived in Oregon City on March 2, 1849. The United States was no longer more than 1,000 miles to the east.

During 1849, even though the great bulk of the St. Paul male population had left for the gold fields, James McKay stayed in St. Paul and operated his Mission Mills night and day. The demand for flour and lumber seemed almost impossible to meet and their prices had soared.

During 1849, several of the immigrant families' children were baptized in the St. Paul church. On January 9, Hugh Cosgrove, son of the Hugh Cosgroves, was baptized. On March 25, Francois Lambert, son of the Augustin Lamberts, a Canadian immigrant family from Montreal, was baptized. William McKay, son of the James McKays, was born on December 30 and baptized the same day. On May 13, while James Coleman was in California, his daughter Catherine Ann, who had been born in Iowa and had come across the plains as a baby two years earlier, was baptized. She was the first daughter of American immigrants to be baptized in the new brick Catholic church.

The Jesuits, seeing the effect that gold was having on California, decided to withdraw from missionary work in Oregon. They closed St. Francis Xavier Mission at St. Paul in 1849. Father Accolti and Father Nobili, who had been operating the Jesuit Mission, left for California on December 10, 1849. They left their property in charge of a caretaker. On arriving in California they formed a Jesuit Province and took over an ailing school near San Jose. They named the school University of Santa Clara.

The closing of St. Joseph's College and St. Francis Xavier Mission, and the partial closing of the Sisters of Notre Dame School in the 1848-1849 period, together with the movement of Archbishop Blanchet's residence from St. Paul to Oregon City in December 1848, greatly reduced the stature of St. Paul. But because it had been the de facto headquarters of the Catholic Church in the Oregon Country for about ten years, the plans and decisions made in St. Paul contributed greatly to the civilization which exists in the Pacific Northwest today.

Ploughing with a Team of Horses

Helen Austin Collection

CHAPTER 7

STAGECOACHES AND STEAMBOATS

The American immigration to Oregon in 1850 was almost zero. People were still flocking directly to California in almost unbelievable numbers.

The Territorial Government passed a law which allowed a married couple to have a 640 acre land claim but limited single men to 320 acres. At that time men outnumbered women by almost 9 to 1 in the Oregon Territory. As a result of this girls as young as 12 and 13 were getting married.

Because of the great demand for Willamette Valley products and the increasing American settlements further upstream on the Willamette River and its tributaries, the number of flatboats and keelboats delivering produce down the river to Canemah was steadily increasing. During the fall months especially, boat traffic on the Willamette below St. Paul was very busy.

In 1850, Charles F. Ray, 21, a native of Sarasota County, New York, arrived in St. Paul. For about a year he operated the Deguire Ferry. That same year he bought the Oregon City-Salem mail route, which was then the only wheeled mail route in the Oregon Territory. His Conestoga Wagon passed through Champoeg and St. Paul on each trip.

About this time George Aplin, a native of England, who had been employed by the Hudson's Bay Company, settled on a farm about a mile and a half north of St. Paul. His wife Marie was the daughter of Peter Wagner, another former Hudson's Bay Company employee, who had a farm just north of Mr. Aplin's farm.

During 1850, the Territorial Government authorized the surveying and building of a road from Salem to Champoeg. The road, which was to pass through St. Paul, became known as the Salem-St. Paul-Champoeg stage road.

In March 1850, Matthew McCormick, 29, from County Meath, Ireland, and Johanna (Clancy) McCormick, 27, his wife, arrived in St. Paul after having mined for gold in California. All of their three small children had died while crossing the plains in 1849. They stayed in St. Paul for about a year, then purchased the Larocque land claim about five miles southeast of St. Paul and moved there.

By this time there was a rather large two-story log inn in St. Paul. This inn, which was owned and operated by Louis Pichet, was approximately three miles southeast of St. Paul on Mr. Pichet's property. It was known as "Louis Pichet's Log Inn", and was the stopping place for many people who were passing through or visiting in the St. Paul-St. Louis area.

In August 1850, John Johnston, 23, a native of County Tyrone, Ireland, arrived in St. Paul and went to work at the Mission Mills. He had come to St. Louis, Missouri with his parents when he was seven years old; and when he was fifteen he and his brother had started working in a flour mill in Beardstown, Illinois. He and two friends, Horace Hill and Don Riddle, had crossed the plains in an ox-drawn covered wagon in 1850. After working at the Mission Mills for about a year he left for the California gold fields.

During the period August 1850 to September 1851, five girls who were to play prominent roles in the St. Paul community for the next fifty years were born. They were Emelie Caroline Raymond, daughter of the Augustin Raymonds; Mary Coleman, daughter of the James Colemans; Marguerite Pichet, daughter of the Louis Pichets; Marguerite Liard, daughter of the Thomas Liards; and Mary McKay, daughter of the James McKays.

In January 1851, Mr. and Mrs. Hugh Cosgrove and their two sons returned to St. Paul from Sacramento, where they had operated a mercantile store and made $15,000 in twenty months. They had taken the $15,000 in gold nuggets and gold dust to San Francisco and purchased $15,000 worth of goods and supplies, which they then brought by steamship to Oregon City and by riverboats to St. Paul. They opened a general store on their property. Shortly after they returned, a daughter, Marie Emaline Cosgrove, was born. She was later to attend Willamette University and play a prominent role in the social affairs of Salem for many years.

On February 24, 1851, the eldest Cosgrove daughter, Marguerite, was married in the St. Paul church to Theodore

Poujade, son of one of the leading doctors on French Prairie. Dr. Poujade, who was a native of France, lived in St. Louis, Oregon.

In August of 1851, Matthew O'Connell Murphy, 21, arrived in St. Paul with his parents and two younger brothers, Daniel and Peter. Because of Matthew Murphy's grandfather's involvement in the Wexford Rebellion of 1798 in Ireland, the family had come to the United States and settled in St. Louis, Missouri. Matthew Murphy had come to the California gold fields in 1849, and had returned to St. Louis in 1851. He and his family came to St. Paul via the Isthmus of Panama. Young Matthew took up a 320 acre donation land claim about one mile north of the mission. His father and mother, Mr. and Mrs. Dan Murphy, took up a 640 acre donation land claim just north of Matthew's claim.

On September 29, 1851, Narcisse Cornoyer, son of Narcisse Cornoyer, a native of St. Clair County, Illinois, and Marie (Bernier) Cornoyer of St. Paul, and Sophie Belleque, daughter of the Pierre Belleques, were married in St. Paul. Narcisse Cornoyer had been a major in the Oregon Army in the Cayuse Indian War and later was to become sheriff of Marion County.

In December 1851, John Gearin, 43, of County Kerry, Ireland, and his wife Ellen (Burns) (Costello) Gearin, 44, a native of County Westmeath, Ireland, and a sister of the Hugh Burns who came to Oregon in 1842, arrived in St. Paul. They both had had previous marriages and had crossed the plains from Fort Wayne, Indiana. They purchased 320 acres of the Belleque land claim about three miles north of St. Paul from Casmir Guardupuis, who had married Mrs. Belleque after Mr. Belleque's death. The Gearins built a log house for themselves and their six children.

In 1851, the sound of steamboat whistles heralded a new era for the entire Willamette Valley above the Oregon City Falls. Steamboats began operating above the falls, travelling as far up the river as Corvallis. By the end of the year there were four operating: the HOOSIER, the CANEMAH, the MULTNOMAH, and the WASHINGTON. The CANE-

S. S. MULTNOMAH—1851

MAH, with two 30-horsepower engines, had a 135-foot length, a 19-foot beam and a 4-foot hold. It contained a travelling post office. This coming of steamboats truly changed life in the St. Paul area. Steamboats docked at the Deguire and Mission Landings on a regular schedule. The population found it much easier to get produce to Oregon City and beyond, and they could now easily visit friends and relatives anywhere along the river from Portland to Corvallis.

The St. Paul area residents met many challenges in their relatively prosperous community. The families were still churning their own butter, making their own candles, sewing their own clothes from goods which could be purchased, splitting rails by the thousands for rail fences, and digging their own wells. There were great hardships and most families lived in log houses. Because of the great demand for their produce due to the California gold rush and the 1851 discovery of gold in Jackson County, Oregon, everyone was busy trying to produce as much as possible. The ratio between the French Canadian-Indian families and the American immigrant families was beginning to change. When the Americans arrived they either took a claim on unclaimed land or purchased part or all of a French Canadian land claim. Apparently the French Canadians were quite willing to sell land, especially at the high prices that were being offered by the Americans. The pattern was to continue for many years. An independent spirit, a friendly nature and a sense of humor were becoming established as part of the character of the community throughout these early years. Gold rushes, ferries, flatboats, keelboats, steamboats and a railroad were to come and go; but the character and personality of the St. Paul community were to remain.

The mantel in the George Eberhard house about four miles north of St. Paul. The mantel was originally in the Henry House on the Willamette Post, where George and Louisa (Jones) Eberhard lived after they were married in 1865. The mantel may have been in the Henry House as early as 1813.

Helen Austin Collection

CHAPTER 8

AN EXPANDING ECONOMY

By 1852, the large landowners in the St. Paul area included the St. Paul Mission, the Jesuit Priests, Jacques Servant, Cuthbert Lambert, Laurant Sauvie, J. B. Deguire, Jean Jeangras, Hugh Cosgrove, Daniel Murphy, Matthew Murphy, Adolph Chamberlain, Louis Pichet, James McKay, John Kennedy, Barney Kennedy, John Johnston, Catherine Challifoix, Louis Bergevin, Pierre Lacourse, David Mongrain, Hercules Lebrun, Francois Bernier, Theodore Gervais, Dr. James Scheil's heirs, Robert Keaton, Thomas Liard's heirs, Patrick Hickey, Peter Clary, Augustin Raymond, George Aplin, William Classens, Michael Coyle, Pierre Belleque and Etienne Lucier.

In 1852, the Notre Dame Sisters' school, which had been operating in a reduced fashion since 1849, was closed completely when the remaining sisters left for California.

Charles Ray, who operated the previously mentioned Oregon City-Salem mail route, and Amelia Eyre, the daughter of Miles and Eliza Eyre, natives of Sheffield, England, where they had conducted a cutlery business, were married in 1852. Amelia Eyre had crossed the plains to Oregon in 1843 when she was about 8 years old, and eventually arrived at Fort Vancouver with her mother and a brother and sister after her father had drowned while crossing the Snake River. After living in the Waldo Hills area for about four years, the family returned to Boston via the California gold fields in 1849, and again crossed the plains to Oregon in 1850.

On October 30, 1852, Robert Keaton, about 20, a native of Dublin, Ireland, arrived. He took up a 160 acre land claim about one mile north of the mission.

In the fall of 1852, after a successful gold mining venture near Yreka, California, John Johnston returned to St. Paul; and in partnership with William H. West, purchased 490 acres from Matthew McCormick about four miles southeast of the mission. They were both young and single. They started clearing land and did their own housekeeping.

By this time many of the St. Paul residents were trying their luck in the gold fields near Jacksonville, which with a population of 5,000 had become the largest city in Oregon. Flour from the Mission Mills and other foods from St. Paul were being sent there by mule train.

At this time some of the people in the St. Paul area were harvesting their grain by cutting it with a scythe and flailing it. This procedure limited the amount they could produce, as an individual could raise only as much as he and his family could harvest during the harvest season, about 20 days. Outside labor was limited, because those who were not in the gold fields were harvesting their own crop. After the harvest the grain was either stored on the farm, shipped down the river or taken to the Mission Mill. Most residents were living in their original log houses, but a few families were building new board houses as lumber became more available.

On February 1, 1853, Honore Picard, a native of Canada, married Mrs. Celeste (Rocbrune) Liard, widow of Thomas Liard.

Later in the year, Father Bartholomew DeLorme, who had accompanied the Catholic Brigade to the California gold fields, was appointed pastor of the St. Paul church. On March 19, the St. Paul community lost one of its original leaders when Etienne Lucier died at the age of 60. The spring flood of the Willamette River covered the St. Paul lowlands and completely washed out Multnomah City. Salem, which was only 20 miles away, replaced Oregon City as the state capital; and in the fall a large warehouse was opened at Fairfield Landing, about 6 miles south of St. Paul.

On October 27, Mary Cosgrove, one of the Cosgrove twins, married James Costello, a son of Mrs. John Gearin by her first marriage. Costello was the Postmaster at Champoeg and also had a store there. Their daughter Mary Ann was born in 1854. She was later to become Sr. Mary James of the Holy Names Sisters.

By the end of the year 1853, the ratio of American immigrant families to the French Canadian-Indian families in the St. Paul area was changing rapidly. This was mainly

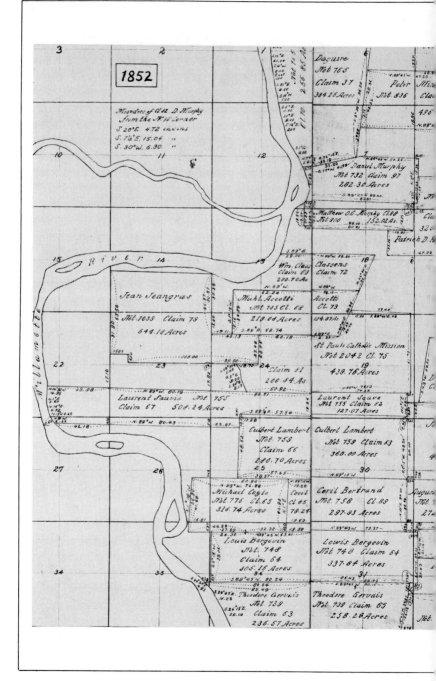

1852

John Garino
Nôt. 874
Claim 70
320.00 As.

Joseph Desp... Claim 33
Nôt. 766 472.34 Acres

Robert Roy 203.73
Nôt. 749 Claim 42 22.84

Andrew Linclain
Nôt. 749 Claim ...
557.28 Acres

Robert Newell
Nôt. 771 Claim 43
640.00 Acres

Peter Papin
Nôt. 747 Claim 85
385.33 Acres

John B. Goodell
Nôt. 762
Claim 91
350.59 As.

Robert ...
Nôt. ...

Adolphus Chamberlain
Nôt. 880
Claim 84
635.02 Acres

Mr. LaForte
330.84 Acres

Etienne Poitier
... Acres

Alphonso Rhoades
Nôt. 742
Claim 101
250.80 As.

George Rhoades
Nôt. 751

Cla...
508...

Hugh Cosgrove
Nôt. 775 Claim 99
642.43 Acres

William ...

James McKay
Nôt. 734 Claim 83
620.67 Acres

Barney Kennedy
Nôt. 750
Claim 48
539.08 Acres
Cert. 156

Claim
558...

Nôt. 779
Claim 86

Tamis Leard dec'd Nôt. 963
Claim 95 263.53 Acres

John Kennedy
Nôt. 752 Cl. 49
317.33 As.

Peter Ga...
Nôt. ...
Cla...
324

Hercules Lebrun Nôt. 746
Claim 59 289.00 Acres

Joseph Barnabie
Nôt. 736
Claim 50
442.43 As.

Jerome B. Jackson
Nôt. 777
Claim 51
320.48 As.

David Mongran
Claim 58 241.08 As.

Nôt. 756

Nôt. 753
Cl. 53

Andrew Bower
238.30 As.

Louis Pichet
Nôt. 745 Claim 57
406.96 Acres

Peter Parisean
Nôt. 770 Cl. 88
371.73 As.

Thomas Hun...

Cl. 54
Nôt. 744
2.50 30 Acres

...rnier
Nôt. 738
325.81 Acres

John Johnson

Eli Gigere
Nôt. 731 Cl. 8...
456.96 Acres

Nôt. 754
425.63 Acres

William West
Nôt. 818 Claim 87
240.20 As.

Mathew McCormick
Nôt. 1095 Claim 90
373.60 As.

Challafoix
433.78 Acres

Silvain Bourgean
Nôt. 769 Cl. 68 305.72 As.

due to two things. First, the French Canadian-Indian descendants had almost no resistance to contagious diseases such as yellow fever, measles, tuberculosis and diphtheria; as evidenced by the great number who died during the trip to the gold fields. Secondly, the American immigrants in general had more money—much of this from success in the gold fields—and, excepting for a few French Canadian-Indian families, they were more interested in obtaining land, which the French Canadian-Indian families were willing to sell for the relatively high prices the American immigrants were offering.

The Cosgrove family can look back at an interesting and amusing incident during the year 1854. After returning from the gold fields Hugh Cosgrove had co-signed a note for one of his friends without telling his wife. When in 1854 he finally knew that his friend was broke, and that he, Hugh, would have to make good on the $7,000 note, he realized that it would break him financially because all of his extra money was tied up in goods in his store. At this point he decided that he would have to tell his wife. When he did she suggested that she might be able to help him. She left for a few minutes and came back with three buckets of gold nuggets and gold dust worth slightly over $7,000, which she had hidden away. Hugh was greatly surprised and relieved.

In 1855, John Hofer, his wife Annie (Zorn) Hofer, and Casper Zorn, natives of Hesse, Germany, who had been living in Baraboo, Wisconsin for several years, arrived and opened a bowling alley at Champoeg. John Hofer was also a cabinet maker and carpenter. Annie and Casper Zorn's father, mother, and their brother Adam were to arrive about two years later.

On October 15, 1855, Miles McDonald, 45, one of the first American immigrants to settle in St. Paul, and Maria Galloway, 21, of Amity, Oregon, were married in St. Paul. Maria was the daughter of the Charles Galloways who had left Hampshire County, Virginia and crossed the plains to Oregon in 1852. The Galloways had a farm in Yamhill County. Maria's paternal grandfather, as a soldier in the Revolutionary War, had been present at Yorktown and saw Cornwallis surrender to George Washington. The McDonalds were later to return to St. Paul and purchase a farm adjoining the mission.

An Indian war started in southern Oregon in 1855. This war was to continue in varying degrees until 1877. As a result of this uprising the United States stationed troops at Fort Yamhill under Lieutenant Philip Sheridan and the Grande Ronde Indian Reservation was established. Eventually about 1,500 Indians from 12 tribes were placed there.

Father O'Reilly replaced Father DeLorme as pastor of the St. Paul church in late 1855.

With the great demand for food and lumber because of the various gold strikes and the rapidly increasing population on the Pacific Coast, it was obvious to the people of St. Paul that it would be very profitable to expand their capacity to meet the growing demand for their commodities. Of utmost importance in accomplishing increased production were large work horses. These horses weighed about 1,500 pounds. They were needed to pull stumps when land was cleared, to plough, to pull other farm implements, to operate the then recently introduced horse-propelled threshing machines, to pull logs to sawmills, and to deliver food and lumber to the markets. All of the farmers raised work horses, and the large-scale farmers eventually used ten to twenty of them. On almost every farm, pasture was abundant on the uncleared part of the property during the spring and summer. But during the winter the horses required a great amount of hay, so large barns became a necessity. Almost all of these early barns were constructed of hewn log beams, wooden pegs to join the beams, and square nails to attach the outer boards. In addition to the need for large barns, an additional need for blacksmith shops developed because of the increased use of mechanical farm implements, which required repair from time to time. Some farmers had small blacksmith shops on their farms.

On February 14, 1856, Matthew Murphy of St. Paul, and Mary Ellen Costello of St. Paul, a native of Fort Wayne, Indiana and a daughter of Mrs. Ellen (Burns) Gearin by her first marriage, were married in the St. Paul church. After the wedding they lived in a small house which Mr. Murphy had built on his property near the river.

On April 7, 1856, Louis Labonte, Jr. and Josette Laframboise were married in St. Paul. He was the son of Louis Labonte, an early Oregon leader mentioned earlier. She was the daughter of Michel Laframboise, one of the most prominent French Canadians in Oregon, who was one of the few survivors of the ill-fated TONQUIN which brought part of the Astor Party to Astoria in 1811. Josette's mother, Emelie (Picard) Laframboise, was a daughter of one of the early settlers in St. Paul, Andre Picard.

After having sold most of the supplies he had purchased in San Francisco in 1851, Hugh Cosgrove closed his store so that he could devote full time to the operation of his farm. Many people who had shopped in his store had come from distant places and often had stayed overnight. One of these had been Aaron Meier, who would later start the Meier and Frank store in Portland. He returned from time to time for an overnight visit, which the young Cosgrove children looked forward to, as he would generally bring them a gift.

A new east-west road which went from what is now the city limits of St. Paul to the Mission Mills was completed by the fall of 1857.

St. Paul residents away from home at a mining camp

Beverly Lambert Bush Collection

CHAPTER 9

STATEHOOD AND
THE OREGON GOLD DISCOVERY

Early in 1857, Green Clay Davidson, about 40, a native of Belleville, Illinois, and his wife Nancy (Million) Davidson, 36, a native of Kentucky, came to St. Paul with their eldest son, William Franklin, 14, and five younger children. In his younger years Green Clay Davidson had been a performer in the circus. The family had crossed the plains to Oregon in 1852. After a short stay in Forest Grove, Oregon, they had moved to Dayton, Oregon, where their operation of a livery stable and mercantile store earned them a great deal of money. When the Davidsons arrived in St. Paul they purchased the J. B. Deguire land claim about two miles northwest of St. Paul. The ferry across the river was located on their new property. They built a store and large warehouse near the ferry landing, as steamboats could dock there. Mr. Davidson called the area near the landing St. Clair, and when a post office was established there in 1859 he was appointed postmaster.

In 1857, Oregon voted 3 to 1 against slavery, which was an important national issue at the time. The issue had special significance to Oregon because the ramifications of the Missouri Compromise of 1850 and the Kansas-Nebraska Act of 1854 had blocked statehood for Oregon. Oregon was a territory, but its residents desired statehood.

Dr. John McLoughlin died at 73 years of age on September 5, 1857. This was a sad event for the people of St. Paul. Many of the French Canadians had worked for him when he was the Oregon Country Manager for the Hudson's Bay Company, and most of the residents knew him personally. He had made it possible for them to start farms and had helped select the site for their mission.

In January 1858, John Cooke, 29, who had first come to St. Paul in 1846, returned from southern Oregon and purchased the Dr. Scheil land claim about 1 mile east of St. Paul.

About this same time, Adolph Jette, 32, a native of
Repentigny, Canada, and a descendant of a very prominent
French Canadian family, arrived in St. Paul. He had come
to Oregon in the early 1850's and mined in the Canyon City,
Oregon area and in Crescent City, California until 1858.
After arriving in St. Paul he lived at the Louis Pichet Log
Inn, purchased a lot near the mission, and built a home for
himself. He then left to prospect for gold in Idaho, spending
most of his time there until 1860.

Oregon finally became a state on Valentine's Day, 1859.
The people of St. Paul and the residents of the rest of Oregon welcomed their new status. During that same year the
steamboat ST. CLAIR, a side-wheeler, was built at Davidson's Landing. It was later to be the only steamboat that
would successfully make the trip over the falls at Oregon
City. The feat was safely accomplished during the flood
of 1861.

On July 25, 1859, Amadee Choquette, a native of St.
Gregoire, Montreal District, Canada, who had come to St.
Paul in the late 1850's, married Marie Bernier of St. Louis,
Oregon. She was born in St. Paul and was the daughter of
the Francois Berniers.

On the 18th and 19th of August, 1859, the people of St.
Paul were startled to see that Mt. Hood seemed to be constantly enshrouded with a silver cloud. After several days

Rail Fence

Alfred Jones Collection

they learned that part of the mountain had been destroyed due to a volcanic eruption.

In 1859, Father Fabian Malo was appointed pastor of the St. Paul church. On Christmas Eve of 1859, Mrs. Thomas Mullen, about 45, and her son Patrick, 20, who was born in County Donegal, Ireland, arrived in St. Paul. They stayed in a small log house with Robert Keaton, who was Mrs. Mullen's son by a previous marriage. Mr. Keaton had a farm about one mile north of the mission.

On January 9, 1860, Mary (Cosgrove) Costello, daughter of the Hugh Cosgroves, whose husband James Costello had died, married Jerome Jackson in Gervais. Jerome Jackson was a cousin of President Andrew Jackson and had come to Oregon in 1839 via Cape Horn when he was 15 years old. After the wedding the Jacksons lived on Mr. Jackson's 420 acre donation land claim near Butteville.

About the same time, James Coleman, who had come to St. Paul in 1847, sold his farm in Yamhill County and bought 320 acres about 2 miles south of St. Paul. He grazed cattle on his new ranch but did not live there.

Gold was discovered in Idaho and eastern Oregon in 1860. Many St. Paul residents left for the new gold fields. The demand for St. Paul's food, lumber and other supplies grew enormously. By this time the Mission Mills were producing about 100 barrels of flour a day. Vast quantities of it were being transported by mule train and steamboat to the new mines.

On April 18, 1860, a devastating Willamette River flood struck the St. Paul area residents who lived closest to the river. Mrs. Matthew Murphy was rescued from a second story window on a mattress with her two-day-old baby, Daniel, in her arms. The Murphys lost practically all their possessions, including almost all of their livestock. During the summer of 1860, Matthew Murphy was appointed Assistant United States Surveyor to conduct surveys of the Washington Territory. When the surveying party was surrounded by Indians in the Seattle area and Chief Surveyor Thomas Hunt was killed, Mr. Murphy became the surveying party chief. Afterwards, he continued to conduct land surveys for the state of Oregon for many years.

The St. Paul Public Grade School was officially established on August 6, 1860. Mr. Adolph Chamberlain, a former Hudson's Bay Company employee who came to St. Paul
about 1840 and had a large farm about 3 miles northeast
of the mission, was the school clerk. In 1856, there was
some informal type of public grade school, as Mr. A. Chamberlain is listed as the school clerk at that time. Mr. John
Cooke was clerk in 1861, by which time school enrollment
at the St. Paul school was 140. At this time the Champoeg
school enrollment was 60, Fairfield was 34 and Arbor
Grove was 53.

On September 11, 1860, John Cooke, 31, of St. Paul, and
Bridget Lee, 29, a native of County Westmeath, Ireland,
were married in the St. Paul church. Bridget Lee was a
second cousin of General Robert E. Lee. She had come to
Oregon in 1855 and had been staying with her aunt, Mrs.
John Gearin, while in St. Paul and with her uncle, Hugh
Burns, when in Oregon City. After the wedding the Cookes
lived in a small log house on Mr. Cooke's farm.

On September 13, 1860, the elder Louis Labonte died.
He had been one of the original French Canadian leaders on
French Prairie and had lived just across the river in Yamhill
County since 1833. Four days later, two natives of France,
Louis Simon and Anne Langres, were married in the St.
Paul church.

In October 1860, Daniel Kavanaugh, 29, a native of
Dublin, Ireland, and his wife, Catherine (Doyle) Kavanaugh, 23, arrived. Mr. Kavanaugh had driven supply
trains from 1850 to 1859 for the United States government
from the middle west across the plains to Fort Laramie and
Fort Bridger, and had once been rescued by Brigham Young
while snowbound. The couple had married in Wisconsin in
1860 and had come to Oregon via the Isthmus of Panama.
They purchased a small farm about 8 miles southeast of
St. Paul.

CHAPTER 10

ST. PAUL ACADEMY AND
THE BIG FLOOD OF 1861

On January 8, 1861, Dieu Donne Manegre, 30, and Emelie Pichet, 16, were married in St. Paul. Dieu Donne Manegre, a native of Winnepeg, Canada, had come to St. Paul in 1856 via Cape Horn and the California gold fields. Emelie Pichet was a daughter of the Louis Pichets.

On February 1, 1861, an event occurred that was to have a great impact on St. Paul for many years. On that date, Father Malo greeted Archbishop Blanchet when, accompanied by three Sisters of the Holy Names of Jesus and Mary, he arrived to open St. Paul Academy, a Catholic elementary school for girls. The women were members of the group of twelve Sisters of the Holy Names who had arrived in Portland from Montreal on October 21, 1859. The year of their arrival this group had opened a Catholic high school for girls in Portland, St. Mary's Academy. The school in St. Paul would enroll both boarders and day students. The Northwest Provincial Superior, Sister Alphonsus de Liguori, arrived with Sister Mary Febronia, who was to be the Superior at St. Paul Academy, and Sister Mary of Mercy, who was to be the assistant. When they arrived in St. Paul the archbishop asked the nuns "to help restore this place to its former prosperity".

Material in the Holy Names Sisters' *Chronicles of the House of St. Paul* reveals much about life in St. Paul at the time. These records show that in 1860, when the nuns had first come to St. Paul to plan for the school, they had decided to have their school and convent in a building which had been the chapel of the Sisters of Notre Dame until they left for California in 1852. At the time of the survey the sisters observed that the building which had been St. Joseph's College was in ruins, and that the interior of the brick church had not been completed. They discovered that an Irish Catholic family with five children was living in a chapel building built by the Jesuits. The family was acting as caretakers for the Jesuits' property, and the Jesuits visited there from time to time. In 1860, the Sisters of the Holy Names had decided that the former Notre Dame Sisters' chapel building would be their home and school. The building was 60 feet by 90 feet and had a steeple but no bell. The sisters arranged for the interior of the structure to have three floors. The first floor was to contain a parlor, refectory, recreation room and hall; the second floor would include a community room, two classrooms and a chapel; and the third floor, which was about ten feet from the ceiling, was to be used as a dormitory. A kitchen, pantry, bakery and cellar were to be in one of the wings which had been the Sisters of Notre Dame boarding school. A building 60 by 30 feet, which appeared to have been constructed of rough lumber which had been blackened by time, had been abandoned. Another wing had been demolished.

The archbishop gave the sisters the buildings and ten acres of land which surrounded them. The planned renovation of the buildings was only partially complete when the sisters arrived in February 1861.

When school opened on February 8, a few boarders had arrived at the St. Paul Academy. The tuition fee was $30 per term, $10 to be paid in cash and the remaining $20 to be paid in provisions. The cash payment was reduced to $5 for girls whose parents had contributed toward the renovation of the building. Most of the students were descended from French Canadian-Indian families but there were a few children of American immigrants. On March 1, Mr. Julien Provost of St. Paul presented the sisters with a statue of St. Joseph which the Sisters of Notre Dame had given to him. On April 1, with the help of the students, the nuns planted 200 apple trees. On April 18, an additional staff member, Sister Mary Agatha, arrived. On June 10, the convent's Indian servant, Indian Jack, left with a load of vegetables for St. Mary's Academy in Portland, which sorely needed them. On June 30, the semester ended. The French Canadian-Indian girls were finding it difficult to learn English but were making progress. As school closed there were three nuns, seventeen boarders and fifteen day students. The following day the nuns went to Portland for

Sister Mary Febronia

Archives Services, Sisters of the Holy Names

St. Paul Academy—1861

Archives Services, Sisters of the Holy Names

a ten-day retreat, leaving Indian Jack in charge of their property. For these women, and the community of St. Paul, the preceding five months had proved challenging yet rewarding.

With the growing number of farms in the St. Paul area, and the discovery of gold in Idaho and eastern Oregon, the production of wheat and oats had increased greatly. James McKay decided to renovate and enlarge the Mission Flour Mill. After the renovation the mill was a two-bur mill and could produce 200 barrels of flour a day, making it one of the two largest flour mills in Marion County. The renovation was well timed. During the period 1861-1867 the Northwest mines were to produce $140 million in gold, which compared favorably with California's $210 million during the same period. The large number of people engaged in mining this Northwest gold caused a tremendous demand for everything produced in the Northwest.

Unusually heavy rains started falling during the last week of November 1861. The rain came down in torrents almost constantly for two weeks, raising the Willamette River higher than anybody had ever seen it, flooding the lowlands and obliterating the falls at Oregon City. The flood caused great loss of life throughout the Willamette Valley. Champoeg, which had been the largest settlement near St. Paul, was completely washed away. The Davidson warehouse, which contained 20,000 bushels of grain which was to be shipped to the mines in Idaho and eastern Oregon, was carried away by the flood. It was commonplace to see entire houses, some with people in them, floating down the river. The swiftness of the current made rescue extremely difficult and in some cases impossible. Many St. Paul area residents were spared because they had moved away from the river after the April 1860 flood. The heavy rains were followed by the coldest weather experienced in the area since the arrival of the explorers and fur trappers fifty years earlier.

After the destruction of Champoeg, St. Paul became the largest settlement in the northern part of French Prairie. The great flood taught the citizens of the Willamette Valley that it was exceedingly dangerous to live on the lowlands along the river.

CHAPTER 11

A DECADE OF SOCIAL AND TECHNOLOGICAL PROGRESS

Early in 1862, Sister Mary of Mercy was named superior of St. Paul Academy. On January 9, when the outgoing superior, Sister Febronia, left St. Paul with a nine-year-old Indian girl, the snow was 24 inches deep. By the 13th of January, the cold weather had caused the two sisters and 17 boarders at the academy to hold classes, eat and sleep in one room in order to keep from freezing. Indian Jack was making bread from frozen leaven and the firewood was covered with snow and ice. The bitterly cold weather was getting worse. The sisters would have preferred to send the children home, but as they were from various places in Oregon and Washington, this was not possible. When there was no more firewood, all clothes were put on top of the blankets. A Miss McCormick, one of the boarders, became very ill. By January 22, there was still no letup to the bitterly cold weather. By January 28, the Willamette River was frozen over, and the sisters were afraid they would not survive. On February 7, Mother Alphonsus came from Portland to take the sisters and students there. On February 12, after arrangements for sleds had been made with the local farmers, school was closed and the sisters and students left for Portland. They arrived in Portland on February 13 after staying overnight in Oregon City. They did not return to St. Paul until March 30. School reopened on April 2. When school closed on July 10, there were two nuns, 30 boarders and 20 day students. The sisters went to Portland for their annual retreat and again left Indian Jack in charge.

In early 1862, James Coleman sold the 320 acre cattle ranch that he had purchased two years earlier. He then purchased 920 acres about a mile south of St. Paul. This had been part of the Cuthbert Lambert and Laurant Sauvie land claims. About this time, Green Clay Davidson, who had lost almost all his possessions in the 1861 flood, opened a mercantile store in Fairfield.

The public grade school building in St. Paul was completed in 1863. The value of the building was $250.

When gold was discovered in Idaho, Casper Zorn and C. W. King, who had been a teacher at Champoeg and was later to be one of the founders of Olds, Wortman and King in Portland, left for Idaho and established a hotel there. Casper Zorn returned in 1862 after having made considerable money from the venture. Mr. Zorn and his brother-in-law, John Hofer, then purchased the Champoeg mill, which had received extensive flood damage. They set about making the many repairs which were necessary before the mill could operate again. The mill was practically all that was left of the original Champoeg.

In July 1863, Dr. John Brentano, 43, and his wife, Elizabeth (Muller) Brentano, 45, natives of Gronnigen, Kingdom of the Netherlands, and their two young sons, arrived in St. Paul. Dr. Brentano was a general practitioner but was also a specialist in obstetrics. He had received his training in the Netherlands and had practiced medicine for five years in Atchison, Kansas. The Brentanos had crossed the plains by ox-drawn covered wagon in 1862, and after staying in Willows, California for about six months, came to St. Paul. They purchased a 700 acre farm about a mile and a half west of the mission, and Dr. Brentano opened a small office in St. Paul.

On May 24, 1864, William Franklin Davidson, 21, son of the Green Clay Davidsons, and Anna Coleman, 18, daughter of the James Colemans, were married in St. Paul. In 1867, they purchased a 320 acre farm about two miles east of the mission. On October 25, 1864, five pupils at the academy had scarlet fever. Mary and Alice Dunn of Josephine County were seriously ill. By December 1, all had recovered.

By 1865, the northwest gold boom was slowing down, and many of the St. Paul residents who had been prospecting in Idaho and eastern Oregon were returning.

Augustin Lambert and Pierre Kittson, another prominent Willamette Valley logger, were conducting extensive logging operations in the St. Paul area. The area still included a good deal of heavily timbered land, but as each year passed more land was logged and cleared and became available for farming.

Lambert logging launch "Anyhow" pulling logs near St. Paul

Beverly Lambert Bush Collection

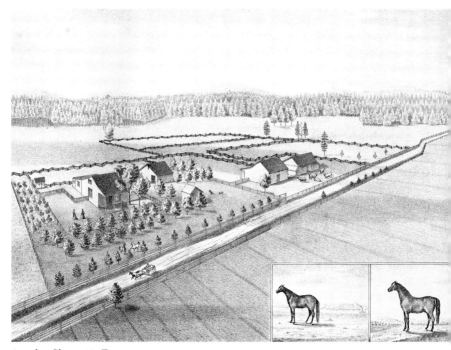

Amadee Choquette Farm

Delight Lorenz Collection

Industrial developments in and beyond St. Paul contributed to the prosperity and stability of the community. Mowing machines were in general use in the early 1860's. Some time prior to 1870, harvesting began to be facilitated by commercial horse-pulled and horse-propelled separators (threshing machines) in the St. Paul area. In John Cooke's diary of October 1870, an item shows that he paid James Coleman $53.75 for harvesting 1,295 bushels of wheat. The threshing machine enabled a greater amount of grain to be raised because it greatly reduced the need for labor at harvest time. The shortage of labor had been a significant factor in limiting production. Not only the quantity being produced but also the quality was being improved. A newspaper article of March 13, 1866, stated, "Mission Flour of Champoeg made by James McKay leads the market just now".

Many citizens in the area were occupied making rails for rail fences, which were gradually honeycombing the St. Paul area. Tens of thousands of rails were required because, besides enclosing the farms, they also divided them into fields. (Approximately 25,000 ten foot long wooden rails were required to enclose a 320 acre farm and divide it into 40 acre fields. Most of the rails were made by sawing fir trees which were about eight inches in diameter into ten foot lengths, and then splitting them lengthwise with an ax into four pieces called rails.)

By this time Hugh Cosgrove had a brick making plant on his farm and, according to the accounts of John Cooke, Mr. Waring of St. Paul was making square-headed nails. (In 1872, Mr. Waring was to make 5,000 square-headed nails for Mr. Cooke.)

An item in the Holy Names Sisters' records tells of a rather tragic incident. On April 3, 1866, a group of girls from St. Paul Academy were playing on a swing called a "dutch horse" on the public grade school grounds. Annie Costello and Wilhelmina Higly were thrown to the ground by the falling of a 1,000 pound log, and Annie suffered a severely broken ankle. Her foot was almost separated from her leg. Wilhelmina had three ribs broken. Dr. Brentano was called and he immediately sent a runner to Champoeg to request

Annie Costello

Dr. Bailey's assistance with the Costello girl's leg. Realizing that the leg might have to be amputated, Annie promised that she would dedicate her life to Christ by joining the Holy Names order if her leg was saved. The doctors decided to try to save her leg. After three months of great pain Annie's leg was almost completely normal again. Eventually she became Sr. Mary James.

In the fall of 1866, Francis Smith, 40, a native of County Cavan, Ireland, his wife Ellen (Nolan) Smith, 24, who was born in County Kilkenny, Ireland, and their two young sons, Charles and Bernard, arrived in St. Paul. The Smiths had been married in Dubuque, Iowa and had lived there until 1863. At that time Francis Smith had received a notice to report for duty in the Civil War. He paid a man to take his place and decided to come west. The Smiths came to San Francisco via the Isthmus of Panama. They took up a land claim which is today part of Golden Gate Park in San Francisco. After about a year they sold the claim and drove a herd of horses to Corvallis, Oregon. After living in Corvallis for about a year they decided to come to St. Paul. The Smiths purchased a 200 acre farm about two and one-half miles northeast of St. Paul where they decided to specialize in the raising of beef cattle.

Later in 1866, Mr. and Mrs. Maurice Scollard, natives of County Donegal, Ireland, and several of their teen-age children, arrived. They purchased a farm about five miles southeast of St. Paul.

By 1866, several of the residents of St. Paul had fairly large homes. They were built of lumber rather than brick because lumber was so readily available. By this time, not only were local sawmills operating but, as previously mentioned, square-headed nails were being made in St. Paul. The large houses became the center of social life. The local young people would arrive at a home late Saturday afternoon and would have dinner in the early evening. About 10:00 P.M. they would start dancing, continuing until about 3:00 A.M. The next morning they would go to church. After having the noon meal and socializing they would return to their homes Sunday evening. The various families would take turns hosting these parties.

The mission and some of the farms had baseball diamonds where people would gather to play baseball, pitch horseshoes, have foot races and pole vault. Almost everybody was interested in horses and horse racing. Amadee Choquette had a stock farm and bred trotting horses. Two of the best were "Emigrant" and "Champoeg". Most of the residents rode horses. Many evenings individuals would ride to a neighbor's place and spend several hours visiting. So, although everyone had to work hard, they found much to enjoy in their community.

At this time there were still some native Calapooian Indians living in the St. Paul area. The relationship between them and the residents was a friendly one, but mixing at social affairs was virtually non-existent.

By the middle 1860's, there were some Chinese immigrants in St. Paul "grubbing land", that is, removing the timber and stumps and preparing the land for farming. Many of them had come to the Willamette Valley as the gold boom in southern Oregon slowed down. The Chinese population was to increase gradually until "cheap Chinese labor" became a national issue in the 1880's and 1890's. There were many necessary contacts with the Chinese and as a result some of the people of St. Paul, in addition to being able to speak English, French and Chinook, could also speak a little Chinese.

The St. Paul families were very interested in giving their children good educations, even though the cost of this was considerable. By 1866, John and James Coleman were attending Willamette University. Hugh Gearin was a student at the Catholic seminary in Oregon City, William McKay was attending Santa Clara University, and John Gearin was a student at the University of Notre Dame. Mary McKay, Mary Coleman, and other St. Paul girls were attending St. Mary's Academy in Portland, and Marguerite Liard was attending high school in Vancouver, Washington. She once saw General Ulysses Grant when he was there after the Civil War.

During 1867, the St. Paul Catholic Church and St. Paul Academy buildings were renovated. The Academy sponsored a fair which raised $800 toward the renovation. The pupils of the Academy presented 7 yards of three-ply carpet for the sanctuary of the church.

In the fall of 1867, John Kennedy, 22, who was known as John Kennedy, Jr., and Julia Scollard, 18, were married. He was the eldest son of the Barney Kennedys and had crossed the plains when he was two years old. Julia had crossed the plains when she was 17 with her parents, who had a farm about five miles southeast of St. Paul. After the wedding the couple lived on John Kennedy's farm about three and one half miles east-southeast of St. Paul.

In 1868, Charles Pelland and George Larocque established a large mercantile store about four miles northeast of St. Paul on a bluff above the original location of Champoeg. Mr. Larocque was born in Montreal and had been a trapper, hunter and guide in the Rocky Mountains. After going to California in 1848 and making in excess of $12,000, he had settled in Butteville. With F. X. Matthieu and several others he had established a large flour mill at Oregon City. Mr. Pelland, who had come from Montreal in 1860, had operated a mercantile store in partnership with Mr. Larocque in Oregon City from 1860 until 1868. The new store between Champoeg and St. Paul was one of the largest in the Willamette Valley. The store carried everything from food, cloth and soap to threshing machines.

An interesting, well-kept ledger which was maintained by Adolph Jette, who was a clerk at the store, shows what the pioneer people were buying and selling in the 1870-1871 period.

Wool, $.33 a pound, might be exchanged for a month's supply of necessities. Eggs, $.20 a dozen, were another frequently exchanged commodity. Potatoes, $.50 a bushel, tallow, $.35 a pound, and bacon, $.14 a pound, were also frequently exchanged. A sack of fur gave one customer a credit of $54.97.

Among items purchased at this time by the pound were:

coffee	$ .25	sugar	$ .14
nails	.08	shot	.25
powder	.75	salmon	.07½
tea	1.00	rice	.12½
butter	.25	candles	.25

Items bought by the pair were:

carpet slippers	$1.00	duck pants	$1.25
bear pants	7.50	men's shoes	2.00
socks	.50	drawers	1.00
overalls	1.00	fine boots	5.50
buckskin gloves	1.25	sheep shears	.50
goat shoes	2.00		

Items purchased by the yard were:

ribbon	$ .37	black alpaca	$ .75
calico	.10		

Single items purchased were:

slate	$ .50	slate pencils	$ .12
willow basket	1.00	linen coat	1.00
fancy apron	.50	chamber	1.00
hair net	.50	silk handkerchief	2.00
wool hat	1.50	parasol	1.50
lady's corset	1.00	wooden rake	.75
coal oil with can	.38	broom	.50
lamp chimney	.25	china doll	.50

Six plugs of tobacco cost $1.00, while a bottle of pain killer or hair oil sold for $1.00 each, and a bottle of gargling oil was $.50. Hair nets must have been in vogue, as they were listed frequently.

Sometimes the purchases of a day told of a sad event, as follows:

On May 3, 1871, a Mr. Ritchie bought the following: 4 yards of velvet for $3.00, 12 yards of muslin for $2.40, 4 yards of fringe for $1.50, 1 bolt velvet braid for $1.00, 1 dozen coffin tacks for $.25, 1 dozen coffin screws for $.37, 1 dozen common screws for $.37, and a beaver coat for $18.00.

On Christmas Eve of 1868, four young girls attending St. Paul Academy received their first communion. They were K. Murphy, F. Piette, A. Bonnie and M. Lambert. On December 27, there was a large farewell party for Father Fabian Malo, who had been the St. Paul pastor for nine years. The new pastor was to be Father Bartholomew De-Lorme, who had accompanied the St. Paul group to the gold fields in 1849, and had previously been the pastor from 1853 to 1855.

In 1869, Charles F. Ray, who had previously run the stage coach mail route between Oregon City and Salem, rented the J. B. Deguire donation land claim, which included the ferry and landing. The property had been owned by Green Clay Davidson since 1856, but because of Mr. Davidson's great financial losses suffered in the flood of 1861 he finally sold the property to Charles Ray in 1873. The ferry and landing then became known as "Ray's

Landing". The property included a large rambling house
which Mr. Davidson had built. The boards were about two
inches thick—rough and perhaps hand sawed—and the
house contained a fireplace in the living room and another
in the parlor.

As the 1860's closed, St. Paul, Oregon was a very prosperous community. It attracted a good deal of commercial
trade, but its status as a trade center was to be very much
altered with the arrival of the railroad in the 1870's.

Narcisse Cornoyer smoking the peace pipe with four Indian Chiefs after settling an
Indian uprising in eastern Oregon in 1876.

Lorraine DeMacon Benski Collection

CHAPTER 12

ST. PAUL AS A COMMERCIAL CENTER

In the early spring of 1870, Robert Keaton, a half brother of Patrick Mullen, left for the Idaho mines. No news was ever received from him again, and Patrick Mullen and his mother took charge of Mr. Keaton's farm.

The steeple was added to the St. Paul church in 1870.

On July 25, Sister Febronia, who had been the first superior of St. Paul Academy, returned to that post. On August 6, a fine piano was received, and applications for instructions in music were received by the Academy.

The new Oregon-California Railroad, which was later to become the Southern Pacific Railroad, completed the railroad link between Portland and Salem which had been started in 1868. The railroad tracks passed through the present day cities of Woodburn and Gervais. Woodburn, which was founded in 1871, would have a population of 145 by 1878. The new railroad made it possible for the people of St. Paul to ship their produce to Portland by rail as well as by steamboat.

In 1870, Peter Kirk, 40, a native of County Louth, Ireland, his wife, Margaret (Lyon) Kirk, 38, a native of County Killarney, Ireland, and their seven children, arrived in St. Paul. Mrs. Kirk's mother came with them. Mr. Kirk, who came from Minnesota, had gone to Montana in 1867 and made a small fortune from a shoemaking shop he had established there for miners. He had then returned to Minnesota, sold his farm and brought his family to San Francisco on the new transcontinental railroad which had been completed the previous year. He purchased 345 acres just north of the mission.

In early 1871, Adolph Jette, 46, married Marguerite Liard, 19, of St. Paul. Since returning to St. Paul in 1860,Mr. Jette had been a clerk in the Davidson, Haler and Pelland-Larocque stores.

On June 25, 1871, the installation of the Stations of the Cross in the church was completed and it was announced that they were officially in place. That same month John

Father Bartholomew DeLorme

Father DeLorme came to St. Paul from Avignon, France, and was the second priest ordained in the Oregon Country. He accompanied the Catholic Brigade to the gold fields and was pastor of the St. Paul Catholic Church from 1853 until 1855. In 1871, he was named pastor of the St. Paul Catholic Church for the second time.

St. Paul Mission Historical Society

Gearin of St. Paul graduated from Notre Dame University.

Matthew Connor, 48, a native of Killican, County Westmeath, Ireland, his wife Mary (Lynch) Connor, 49, a native of Reharney, County Westmeath, Ireland, and their eight children, came west on the transcontinental railroad in

1871. They had been neighbors of the Peter Kirks in Minnesota; and Mr. Kirk had purchased the old Jesuit Mission farm, about a mile east of St. Paul, for them. Mission Landing was on their property.

According to stories handed down by the Zorn, Jette and McKay families, some time in the early 1870's a devastating wind or tornado struck the St. Paul area. The storm toppled so many trees that it was almost impossible to get to a neighbor's house. Mary McKay became seriously ill during the storm, but large downed trees blocking the roads made it impossible for her parents to take her to a doctor.

At the graduation ceremony on July 1 and 2, 1872, the students of St. Paul Academy presented a musical recital and a four act play called "The Coronation of Isabella I". The affair showed the community the quality of education taking place at the Academy. According to the *Chronicles of the House of St. Paul* the leading roles were played by Mary Weston, Albina Gratton, Eliza Coleman, Katie McKay, Elizabeth Brummel, Emma Patterson, Mary Lambert, Dorilda Gagnon, Rose Serveney, Bridget McDonald, Leonie Patterson, Salome Raymond, Sydonia Serveney, Magdalene Raymond, Mary Hunt and Ellen Coffee. Others participating were Ellen McDonald, Zenaide Gregoire, Rose Allard, Margaret Marshall, Teresa Nibler, Esther Jackson, Gloria Gratton and Miss Gervais. The piano recital featured Eliza Coleman, Katie McKay, Minnie Murphy and Anna Kennedy. The performance managers were Anna Kennedy, Agnes Nibler and Emma Coleman.

On New Year's Day 1873, Charles Pelland, about 45, and Mary Coleman, 21, were married in St. Paul.

In May 1873, Cyprien Belleque, youngest son of the Pierre Belleques, and Julienne Bergevin, daughter of the Louis Bergevins, were married in the St. Paul church. Cyprien was born shortly before his father died while returning from the gold fields in 1849. The Louis Bergevins, who had a 700 acre farm about three miles south of St. Paul, were one of St. Paul's most prominent families.

In late 1873, Francois Ernst, 33, his wife, Mary (Veser) Ernst, 35, both natives of Colmar, Alsace-Lorraine, and their four children, arrived in St. Paul. Mr. and Mrs. Ernst

First St. Paul Post Office—1874

St. Paul Mission Historical Society

Eldridge Pack Wagons

Eldridge Family Collection

had come west via the Isthmus of Panama in 1869. Mr. Ernst, who had worked as a shoe repairman in Portland, opened a shoe shop in St. Paul.

On June 24, 1874, a U.S. Post Office was established in St. Paul. John F. Theodore Brentano, a son of Dr. Brentano, was appointed as the first postmaster.

Four Corners Public Grade School, about two miles east of St. Paul, was opened in the fall of 1874. Two of the first teachers there were Caledonia "Callie" Orton of Yamhill County and Mary C. "Minnie" Murphy of St. Paul. Both were to be leaders in the social life of the St. Paul community during the 1880's and 1890's.

Andrew Hughes, 30, a native of County Meath, Ireland, his wife Rose (Connor) Hughes, 23, who was born in Freeport, Illinois, and their year-old son, Tom, arrived in St. Paul. They purchased a small farm next to Mrs. Hughes' parents, the Connors. The Connor and Hughes families had been neighbors in Minnesota and Mr. Hughes was an experienced carpenter.

By 1874, the annual church fair was a big social event in the community. At these fairs, foods were donated and sold and local merchants contributed articles which were raffled. The Connor family records show that the Connors won a much prized mahogany rocking chair at one of the fairs.

Much time was spent growing and preserving food. All looked forward to the fun of making sausage in the fall and later the pleasure of eating it because it tasted so good. A typical sausage recipe used by Mrs. William McKay, which she perhaps obtained from her mother, Mrs. Dan Kavanaugh, was as follows:

"A good way to make and keep sausage.

For ten pounds of meat take five tablespoons of sage; four of salt and two of pepper; some add a tablespoon of ginger, and some a little summer savory. When nicely minced, form into patties, fry until nearly done, and pack in stone jars. When entirely cold, completely cover with melted fat, put on a weight, and if kept in a cool place, sausage put up in this manner will keep almost any length of time."

Almost all of the food excepting sugar, salt, coffee, tea and spices was raised on the farms. Life, although enjoyable, was not easy, because so many things had to be done by hand.

In 1874, with the opening of the locks on the west side of the Willamette River at the Oregon City Falls, the St. Paul residents were able to travel the complete distance to Portland on the river without changing steamboats. (The population of Portland was then about 12,000.)

At that time St. Paul had the Catholic church, a Post Office, two stores, St. Paul Academy, a public grade school, an orphanage, a shoe shop, a doctor's office, a blacksmith shop and a saloon.

Sports activities were held on Sundays and holidays at the several baseball diamonds in the area, the circular horse racing track about two miles north of St. Paul, and the straight horse racing track about two miles east.

James and Dan Murphy were attending St. Mary's College, which was then located in San Francisco, and Steve Coleman was attending Willamette University, in 1875. During this same year there was quite an incident at Ray's Landing, where the boiler of the steamboat ELK exploded.

On June 13, 1875, the Gervais Catholic Church was dedicated. The town of Gervais had been established about 1870.

In 1875, a new cemetery, which had its own chapel, was established just east of the mission. The remains of some persons who had been buried in the old cemetery, just northeast of the mission, were moved to the new one.

On November 5, 1876, Thomas Coleman, 22, and Caledonia Orton, about 20, a daughter of Ira and Martha (Burton) Orton of Chehalem Valley, Yamhill County, were married. The couple settled on Mr. Coleman's 160 acre farm about 3 miles northeast of St. Paul. In 1881, they were to build one of the finest homes in the community on their farm. It had a large recreation room on the second floor and became the scene of numerous social activities.

Miles McDonald, who had come to St. Paul in 1846, died in 1876. For a time he had lived in Yamhill County, but he had later moved back to St. Paul and purchased a farm just

Gearin ferry crossing the Willamette

Dr. John Gearin Collection

Sarah Kennedy on her horse

Sarah Kennedy Collection

north of the mission. After Mr. McDonald's death Mrs. McDonald's mother, Mrs. Galloway, stayed with Mrs. McDonald, who operated their farm with the assistance of her six daughters and two young sons.

On New Year's Day 1878, Francois Lambert, 28, of St. Louis, Oregon, and Clementine Mongrain, 22, daughter of the David Mongrains, were married in St. Paul.

In 1878, work was started on the narrow gauge railroad, which was to run on the east side of the river from Ray's Landing to Silverton. Construction began on a bridge across the river, but the idea was abandoned when the bridgehead collapsed. The railroad project employed 1,200 people. St. Paul had three saloons and two breweries at this time. There were many Chinese people in the area, from whom the St. Paul boys were earning "gun money" and "shell money" by shooting wild ducks. It must have been an exciting time for the community.

By 1878, Peter Kirk had constructed a large warehouse about a quarter mile north of St. Paul, and was buying and storing grain. He and his son Emmett also built a merchandise store in St. Paul.

On June 26, 1878, John Gearin, 26, of St. Paul and Matilda Raleigh, 22, of Yamhill County, were married.

In 1879, Adolph Jette purchased the Pelland-Laroque Store and warehouses, where he had been a clerk for ten years. An 1880 Book of Accounts maintained by Mr. Jette shows the prices of some of the items sold.

Hay fork	$1.00	Castoria, bottle	$ .35
Cow bell and strap	1.10	Vanilla, bottle	.25
Rope, foot	.20	Perfume, bottle	.75
Butter ladle	.25	Coal oil, gallon	.50
Curry comb	.40	Ball of candle wick	.10
Ax handle	.40	Coffee, pound	.25
Mink trap (old)	.38	Butter, pound	.25
Coffin	3.00	Rice, pound	.07
Hand saw	2.00	Tea, pound	.55
Well bucket	1.25	Canary seed, pound	.25
Pocket knife	1.25	Honey, 5½ pounds	.68
Monkey wrench	.90	Cod fish, pound	.08
Shearing 31 sheep	1.55	Cheese, pound	.25

Razor	$1.50	Flour, sack	$1.25
Razor strap	1.00	Oatmeal, 10 pounds	.63
Nails, pound	.10	Peaches, #2 can	.40
Skein yarn	.28	Tobacco, plug	.20
Thimble	.10	Merschaum pipe	7.50
Collar buttons	.13	Alaska shoes	2.00
Lining, yard	.25	Suspenders	.50
Ticking	.18	Black straw hat	.75
Lace	.20	White gloves	.37
Veiling	.55	Necktie	.25
Bleached muslin	.14	Leghorn hat	1.50
Ducking	.25	Ventilated garters, pair	.40
Elastic	.13	Mohair coat	2.00
Black muslin	.14	Calf boots, pair	6.00
Cod liver oil, bottle	1.00	Gum coat	4.50
Castor oil, bottle	.50	Gum boots, pair	5.50
Ague cure, bottle	1.00	Duster	1.50
Blood purifier, bottle	1.00	Fiddle strings	.25
Sarsaparilla, bottle	1.00	Eight days' board	6.00
Lard oil, bottle	.25	Coffin handles	2.00
Strychnine, bottle	.50	First grade reader	.25
Hair vigor, bottle	1.00	First grade speller	.25
Soothing syrup, bottle	.25	Third grade reader	.50
Eye water, bottle	.25	Fish hook and line	.25
Bear's oil, bottle	.25	Baby rattle	.20
Wood, cord	2.00		

Mr. Jette also purchased some items from his customers. Prices paid for some of these items were as follows:

Kraut, keg	$3.00	Pork, pound	$ .07
Wheat, bushel	.80	Butter, pound	.20
Oats, bushel	.34	Hide, 52 pounds	2.48
Bacon, pound	.12	Gloves, seven pairs	3.50

Oregon was producing 240,000 pounds of hops annually by 1879. Production of hops, which was to become one of St. Paul's biggest crops, had increased from 10,000 to 240,000 pounds in ten years. Hops and hop driers became part of the St. Paul landscape.

When the Oregonian Railway Company, Ltd. was planning the route from Ray's Landing to Silverton, the plan was for the railroad to go through St. Paul and then either

Hauling Hay

Gerald Connor Family Collection

The James McKay Home

St. Paul Mission Historical Society

through Gervais or Woodburn. A bitter dispute arose between those who favored the route through Gervais and those who favored the route through Woodburn. The case finally went to the Oregon Supreme Court, which decided that the route would be through Woodburn. This decision, together with the fact that the Oregon-California Railroad made it possible for farmers to transport grain and other produce by rail, had a disastrous effect on Fairfield. The Fairfield area population dropped from 822 in 1860 to 613 in 1870, and to 50 by 1879. The Woodburn route decision also had an adverse effect on Gervais, as it made Woodburn a railroad center with both a north-south and an east-west line passing through it. St. Paul was on the east-west railroad line and had north-south river transportation two miles away at Mission Landing and Ray's Landing.

Among the largest landowners in the St. Paul area in 1879 were the St. Paul Mission, August Raymond Heirs, James Coleman, W. F. Davidson and John Coleman, James Mc-Kay, C. L. Bergevin, Dieu Donne Manegre, Amadee Choquette, E. J. Harding, Henry Picard, Hugh Cosgrove, John Cooke, Peter Clary, Andrew Murphy, J. B. P. Piette, T. Wiggins, Frank Smith, L. Prevost, Simon Connor, John D. Kennedy, Dr. John Brentano, J. W. Smyth, Matthew Murphy, George Aplin, Charles F. Ray, Peter Kirk, William Trevor, John Gearin, S. Peletier, Henry Oahslager, Edward Coffee, J. B., L., and A. J. Bergevin, J. Belleque, E. N. Doupierre, James Coyle, Barney Kennedy Estate, John Kennedy, Jr., John Johnson, and Thomas Coleman.

The winter of 1879 was the coldest since 1861, and no winter like it was to occur again until 1919.

The weather-vane rooster on top of the steeple of the St. Paul Catholic Church

CHAPTER 13

THE FRUITS OF SUCCESS

As the 1880's began, St. Paul was still in the grip of the cold weather of the winter of 1879-1880. When the cold spell passed, the construction of the railroad resumed.

Up until about this time, almost all of the people in their twenties and thirties who had been born and raised in St. Paul were descendants of the French Canadians. But by 1880, there were some descendants of American immigrants who had been born and raised in St. Paul, who were in their twenties and thirties. Life was far different than it had been fifty years earlier when there were wolves and even a few grizzly bears in the area. Many French Canadian-Indian families had sold their farms to American immigrants, who made up a majority of the population. The increasing use of binders, threshing machines, other farm implements and sawmills resulted in the operation of commercial and family-owned blacksmith shops. Horses furnished most of the power for farming and logging, and many farmers continued to have ten to twenty large work horses. Patrick Mullen, Amadee Choquette and John Johnston had large horse breeding operations and sold horses throughout the Willamette Valley and beyond. In addition to the large houses which had been built, large barns and large hop driers dotted the landscape. The farmers with small blacksmith shops on their farms reconditioned their farm equipment during wintertime. By 1880, the farming units had changed from small log houses with a few animals and sheds to rather well organized business ventures with facilities for conducting social activities, and many farmers were relatively wealthy.

On October 4, 1880, the narrow gauge railroad made its first run from Ray's Landing to Silverton, and the St. Paul residents were invited to ride on the first trip. Many accepted the invitation. In the festive spirit of the day the young boys, who rode on flat cars and had buckets of small rocks, had a contest to see who could hit the most telegraph poles. R. E. "Emmett" Kirk was appointed St. Paul agent

The narrow gauge railroad's wood burning locomotive

Picking hops at the John Kennedy, Jr. farm

Emmett Kirk's Store

Hazel Kirk Blackerby Collection

Arbor Grove Grade School

Sarah Kennedy Collection

for the railroad. Traffic could now move north and south on the river and east and west on the railroad.

On November 10, 1880, Patrick Mullen, 41, and Mary Ellen Flynn, 25, were married in St. Paul. Miss Flynn's father, who was a native of Ireland, had a farm about 4 miles northeast of St. Paul. After the wedding the couple lived in a new house on Mr. Mullen's farm. Later, one of their sons, Charles Mullen, was one of the leaders in the drive to obtain a high school for St. Paul. When the school opened in 1923, he was chairman of the school board and remained in that position for many years.

In 1881, Adolph Jette purchased Statts' Saloon near his store, and modernized it so that it became one of the finest saloons in Marion County. He sold the old equipment to William Murphy, who started another saloon in St. Paul. Alfred Lambert also had a saloon in St. Paul at this time.

On October 27, 1881, Hugh Gearin, 32, married Mary C. "Minnie" Murphy, 24, in the St. Paul Church. Mr. Gearin was later to be a member of an expedition party—which included Governor Lane's son and friends of Theodore Roosevelt—which explored Alaska and Siberia. Mary C. "Minnie", who had been born and raised in St. Paul, could speak English, French, Chinook and a little Chinese; and had been one of the first teachers at Four Corners Public School. After the wedding the couple moved into Mr. Gearin's two-story mansion. The house was distinguished by the fact that it had a dining room, living room and parlor on each floor, luxurious chandeliers throughout the house, and two large fireplaces on the ground floor. It also had a 30 by 60 foot recreation room on the second floor. It became the scene of many social activities in the 1881-1910 period.

In 1882, the Charles Pellands returned to St. Paul and established a large mercantile store. The Jettes converted one of their large warehouses to a dance hall, which attracted large crowds from as far away as Portland every Saturday night.

During the 1881-1882 period, there were numerous weddings in St. Paul. Some of the young people who were married at this time were John Bergevin and Salome Picard, James Murphy and Elizabeth Kirk, Henri Picard, Jr. and

Cross above Archbishop Blanchet's grave in the St. Paul Catholic cemetery

St. Paul Mission Historical Society

Mary Choquette, John Coleman and Mary Kennedy, John McCormick and Katherine McKay, Eusebe Forcier and Salome Raymond, and William Shaw and Ellen McDonald.

June 21, 1883 was a significant day for the St. Paul community. On that day Archbishop Blanchet was buried in the St. Paul cemetery. Forty-four years earlier the then Father Blanchet had chosen the community as his base of operations for the Catholic Church in the then Oregon Country. Archbishop Blanchet was well known and greatly respected by the community which contained, and was named after, the first Catholic church consecrated in the state of Oregon. On January 13, 1885, William McKay, 35, and Ann Kavanaugh, 20, were married in St. Louis, Oregon. The couple moved into the large two-story house which Mr. McKay had built. It had a recreation room on the second floor and was situated on his 640 acre farm about three miles northeast of St. Paul.

On April 16, 1885, on his 25th birthday, Daniel Murphy, who seven years later was to become United States Attorney for Oregon, and Caroline Kennedy, 20, were married in St. Paul. After the wedding they moved to Portland, where Mr. Murphy had a law practice.

In 1886, some finishing details were added to the St. Paul church. The cost was $2,000. Later, when Father James Rauw was pastor during the 1900-1903 period, the church was thoroughly renovated. The St. Paul church records show that new altars, pews and stained glass windows were installed, the tower was completely remodelled, and a handsome and spacious sacristy was added. The cost of the renovation was about $15,000.

In 1886, two brothers, Alphonse Buyserie, 16, and Isadore (Dory) Buyserie, 14, natives of Grammont, Belgium, arrived in St. Paul and went to work at the Mission Mills. They had arrived at Gervais in 1884 with twenty-five cents between them and had been working at the Benedictine Abbey at Mt. Angel, which had been established in 1882.

In 1887, the Right Reverend F. X. Blanchet, Vicar General of the Catholic Church in Oregon, a nephew of Archbishop Blanchet, was named pastor of the St. Paul parish. Later, in 1887, after operating the Mission Mills in St. Paul for forty years, James McKay decided to retire. He moved into one of Portland's most elegant residence buildings, the Revere House, which was located on property he had purchased from Ladd and Tilton in 1865. The property was situated at the southwest corner of Third and Stark Street. In 1893, he was to renovate the building and add to it. It became the five-story McKay Building, one of Portland's most modern office buildings.

In 1889, Steven Merten and his wife Theresia (Gooding) Merten, both about 40 and natives of Merten, Alsace-Lorraine, arrived with their four daughters and year-old son. They has come from Austin, Nevada, where they had engaged in cattle ranching and mining. They purchased a farm about a half mile south of the church.

Later in 1889, Nicholas Gooding, 57, and his sons John and Charles, arrived in St. Paul. Mr. Gooding had come to Oregon the previous year and had decided to settle in St. Paul. He and his two sons had journeyed from Indiana on the transcontinental railroad and had brought with them a sawmill and a horse-drawn steam-propelled threshing machine. They purchased a 75 acre farm about two and one-half miles southeast of St. Paul. They set up the sawmill on their property and started producing lumber. They also operated the farm and established a commercial threshing machine operation. The next year Mrs. Gooding, who was Stephen Merten's sister, arrived in St. Paul via the transcontinental railroad with the remaining five Gooding children. Shortly thereafter Mr. Gooding built a blacksmith shop, and before long people were saying that Nicholas Gooding could make anything from iron.

In late 1889, the Pellands sold their store to Herman Waltz and Joseph Gooding. The Pellands then purchased a farm about two miles south of St. Paul.

In 1890, during late January and early February, the worst Willamette River flood in the St. Paul area since 1861 occurred. The water was so high that steamboats were docking at Jette's store. The Jettes lost about 2,000 bushels of wheat, and the Zorn sawmill was ruined. The flood did so much damage to Ray's Landing and to the railroad tracks in the lowlands that both were abandoned and discontinued. Thus St. Paul's railroad era came to a disastrous end. Several other ferries which had been damaged were repaired and continued to operate, as that was the only way to Yamhill County. Perhaps the first ferry crossing the Willamette River was established near St. Paul in 1826, yet it was to be nearly 100 years before any bridge was built

The Lambert Hotel

Beverly Lambert Bush Collection

S. S. OREGANO docked at a landing near St. Paul

Gerald Connor Family Collection

Nicholas Gooding's Steam-propelled Threshing Machine

Elmer Gooding Collection

"Donkey" used to pull logs to the loading dock

Jean Abner Collection

across the Willamette River anywhere between Salem and Oregon City. Finally, in 1913, the St. Paul-Newberg bridge was completed and the ferry era in the St. Paul area ended.

By 1890, the horse-propelled threshing machines were disappearing. There were at least six steam-propelled threshing machines in the St. Paul area. Some were moved by horses, and others were moved by steam engine. They were owned by Frank Coleman and James Cooke, Thomas Kerr, Gearin and Pillette, John Kennedy, William McKay and Nicholas Gooding.

The community had a 25 member band which was said to have been one of the better bands in Marion County. Among the members were three Goodings, two Colemans, Bert Pelland, Jack Davidson and John Hughes.

The town also had four baseball teams. Among the better players were Henry and Louis Ernst, Frank Coleman, Alfred Lambert and William Murphy. (In 1905, two of these baseball players, Frank Coleman and William Murphy, would hire the Goerdle Brothers to "grub" some land just south of the city limits for a baseball field. The cleared land became the St. Paul Baseball Field and three boys, Curtis Coleman, Herman Pillette and Ted Pillette, who got their start in baseball there, became major league baseball players. The converted baseball field became St. Paul Rodeo Grounds in 1935.)

Second St. Paul Academy Building—1890

Archive Services, Convent of the Holy Names

A. JETTE.
GEN^{RL.} MERCHANDISE

Jette Store

Frank Jette Collection

Hugh Gearin Home

Dr. John Gearin Collection

Parlor of Gearin Home

Dr. John Gearin Collection

Dining Room of Gearin Home

Dr. John Gearin Collection

Thomas Coleman Home

St. Paul Mission Historical Society

Dieu Donne Manegre Home

Louise Mucken Manegre Collection

Francis Smith Hop Drier

Claude Smith Collection

John Cooke Hop Drier

Jean Abner Collection

CHAPTER 14

EARLY DAY ST. PAUL, OREGON IN PERSPECTIVE

After experiencing the effects of three gold rushes, the various floods, the transition from canoes, flatboats and keelboats to steamboats, and the establishment and demise of the ten-year narrow gauge railroad, the St. Paul residents learned to make great adjustments to changed situations. The resulting philosophy was probably still reflected in 1930,when the St. Paul High School graduating class of that year selected as their school motto "We'll find a path or make one" and as their school song "Keep Your Sunny Side Up".

There are now thousands of descendants of the people who came to St. Paul during the 1820-1890 period. Throughout its existence the St. Paul Catholic Church has been a cohesive and guiding force for the people who have lived there. St. Paul has been a close community, and when somebody had trouble the others pitched in and did what they could to help. Up until 1890, most of the people who grew up in the area stayed there because the land could be divided, and there was plenty for each of the children. Some who grew up in St. Paul and left had distinguished careers. Examples of these are Dan Murphy, who became Chairman of the Democratic Party for Oregon in 1892 and United States Attorney for Oregon in 1893; John Gearin, who became United States Senator from Oregon in 1905; Edward Pillette's son Herman, who, as a pitcher for the Detroit Tigers, was one of the leading pitchers in major league baseball in the early 1920's; Veronica McDonald's daughter Lessie Lind, who married Charley Shea, who later became President of Six Companies, Inc. which built Hoover Dam in the early 1930's; Bernard Krechter and Phillipina (Ernst) Krechter's son Joseph, who played in Paul Whiteman's Band and later arranged music for Bing Crosby; and Joseph Smith's son Leslie, who, as head of the Associated Press in San Francisco, received and distributed the first public news which told the people of the United States that Japan had attacked Pearl Harbor.

Those who stayed in St. Paul continued to operate the farms and other local enterprises and contributed substantially to the culture and commerce of the state of Oregon. Over the years the community gradually changed from the St. Paul Catholic Mission to one of the many typical small towns in the Pacific Northwest—but with a heritage that is unique. This heritage resulted from overcoming tremendous and complicated obstacles, some of which were brought about by great and rapid changes. Its impact has been deep and its influence far-reaching.

The St. Paul Band—1897
Left to right: Fred Horner, Frank Coleman, Louis Vivette, Peter Kirk, Remie Lambert, Charley Kerr, Peter McDonald, Frank McGrath, Band leader Pheifer Teuchen, Thomas Hughes, Jack Kerr, Willie McGrath, Edd Kerr, Fred Davidson, Bert Pelland, James Kerr and Anthime Ernst

St. Paul Mission Historical Society

Sawing firewood on the Kuensting farm about 1910

Charles Johnston Collection

Hop baling scene—1902

Jean Abner Collection

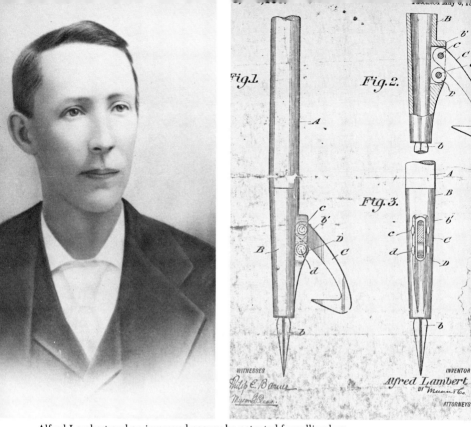

Alfred Lambert and an improved peavey he patented for rolling logs

Beverly Lambert Bush Collection

Logging camp scene near St. Paul

Beverly Lambert Bush Collection

Baling hay with steam power on the Kavanaugh farm in 1912

Clarence Kavanaugh Collection

The Ben Smith Cattle Ranch

Mark Smith Collection

Typical scene in front of the St. Paul Catholic Church—1911

Jean Abner Collection

Krechter Hotel—1902

Jean Abner Collection

Steam-propelled threshing machine in action

Beverly Lambert Bush Collection

Hauling gravel for the new St. Paul Academy after the 1911 fire

F. R. Coleman Collection

Frank Davidson and his horse and buggy—about 1895

St. Paul Mission Historical Society

PART II

THE PIONEER FAMILIES

PIERRE BELLEQUE AND GENEVIEVE (ST. MARTIN) BELLEQUE

Cyprien Belleque, Rosa Belleque and Narcisse Guardupuis

Lorraine DeMacon Benski Collection

Pierre Belleque was born January 9, 1797. He was the son of Louis Belleque and Marguerite (Beaudoin) Belleque of Assumption Parish in the province of Quebec, Canada. In 1820, he came to Oregon with the Northwest Fur Company. He eventually became a middleman and steersman for the Hudson's Bay Company. Sometime between 1830 and 1833, he settled on a land claim about three miles north of present day St. Paul. He was one of the first white settlers on French Prairie.

Genevieve St. Martin was the daughter of Joseph St. Martin, an early fur trapper, and a woman of the Chinook Nation. She was born about 1814.

Pierre Belleque and Genevieve St. Martin were married about 1830. Their marriage was later confirmed in the St. Paul Catholic Mission in 1839.

The Belleques were very much interested in having Catholic priests in the Oregon Country, and particularly in French Prairie. Pierre Belleque, who was fairly well educated by the standards of the time, was one of the leaders in the preparation of the petition which requested priests for the Oregon Country. The first fur trading post in Oregon, which was built by the Northwest Fur Company about 1813, was located on land which became part of the Belleque farm. The Belleques lived in the trading post house, which was constructed of a combination of locally hewn logs, and boards which had come around Cape Horn by steamship. They raised wheat, oats and vegetables and by 1844 they owned about 400 horses, 1,000 cattle, 36 hogs, and numerous sheep. They also possessed 12 clocks and 20 watches.

When Father Blanchet arrived at Fort Vancouver in late 1838, Pierre Belleque and his neighbor Etienne Lucier went to meet him. About two months later these men again went to Fort Vancouver and accompanied Father Blanchet to the mission church on French Prairie. On the day of the first Mass in the St. Paul Catholic Mission church, January 6, 1839, the Belleques' three children were baptized by Father Blanchet. On January 21, 1839, the Belleques were married in the church by Father Blanchet.

Pierre Belleque, accompanied by his 13-year-old son Pierre, went to the California gold fields with the Catholic Brigade in 1849. Before he left he made his will, which was the first recorded will in the Oregon Territory. The Belleques were very successful in California and decided to return to Oregon via steamship from San Francisco. On the return voyage Mr. Belleque became quite ill from a fever contracted in the gold fields. He died before reaching home and was buried at sea near the mouth of the Columbia River in October 1849. Father DeLorme, who was returning to

St. Paul on the same ship, also contracted the fever but survived. Young Pierre returned to St. Paul, but the gold that he and his father had mined was missing. This loss remains a mystery. Mr. Belleque's estate was valued at $3,154.50. It included the land claim, fifty acres of which were enclosed and 45 of which were under cultivation. There were two houses, 700 bushels of wheat, a threshing machine appraised at $400 which was sold for $505 at auction, and numerous farm animals. After Mr. Belleque's death, Mrs. Genevieve Belleque married Casmer Guardupuis of St. Paul. They continued to operate the farm.

Pierre and Genevieve Belleque had seven children: Sophie, who married Narcisse Cornoyer of St. Paul; Pierre II, who married Mary Ann Gagnon of St. Louis, Oregon; Genevieve, who married Felix Gregoire of St. Paul; Esther, who married Joseph Hibert; Joseph, who died when a young boy; Jean Baptiste, who married Victorienne Vassal; and Cyprien, who married Julienne Bergevin of St. Paul. Julienne was a daughter of the Louis Bergevins, who had a large farm about three miles south of St. Paul, and a granddaughter of one of the earliest St. Paul settlers, Jacques Servant.

Mr. Belleque's death at sea took place in 1849 when he was 52. Mrs. Belleque, who later became Mrs. Guardupuis, died in 1904 when she was about 90 years of age.

The Pierre Belleques were important leaders in the establishment of social, religious and economic life in early Oregon. Their children attended St. Joseph's College and the Sisters of Notre Dame School in St. Paul. The family loved social affairs and dancing. Sophie's husband, Narcisse Cornoyer, was a major in the Oregon Volunteers during the Indian War of 1855-56, Indian Agent for the Umatilla Reservation, and sheriff of Marion County from 1856 until 1859. Throughout their lives the Pierre Belleques were generous contributors to the St. Paul Catholic Church and participated in all church activities. In addition to raising their own family they raised an orphan girl, Rose Aucent, who became the wife of F. X. Matthieu of Butteville.

DR. JOHN FREDERICK JOSEPH BRENTANO AND ELIZABETH WILHELMINA J. M. (MULLER) BRENTANO

Dr. and Mrs. John Frederick Joseph Brentano

Harold Brentano Collection

John Frederick Joseph Brentano was born in Gronnigen, Kingdom of the Netherlands, on March 20, 1820. He obtained his Doctorate in Medicine in June 1843 and obtained an advanced degree in Obstetrics in 1844.

Elizabeth Muller was born in Gronnigen on February 19, 1818. On April 16 and 17, 1844, Dr. John Brentano, 24, and Elizabeth Muller, 26, were married in Gronnigen. After the wedding Dr. Brentano practiced medicine in the Netherlands until 1857, by which time the Brentanos had two children, John and Ringner. The two boys were sent to school when four years of age and were given as much education as possible before the family left for the United States in August 1857.

When the Brentanos came to the United States they settled in Atchison, Kansas, where Dr. Brentano resumed his practice of medicine. In the spring of 1862, they crossed the plains by ox-drawn covered wagon. That fall they arrived at Willows, California. The following July, Dr. Brentano, 43, and his wife, Elizabeth, 45, and their family arrived in St. Paul. The Brentanos purchased a 700 acre farm about one and one-half miles west of St. Paul.

Initially Dr. Brentano established his office in St. Paul, but when his house was completed he moved his office to his home. He rode horseback to his various medical calls, which served an area that included St. Paul, Champoeg, Fairfield and St. Louis. Some people paid him in gold dust, the value of which he determined by weighing it on his medical scales. He delivered most of the babies born in the St. Paul area between 1863 and 1900, when he retired at the age of 80. On his farm he established a landing which is known today as San Salvador beach. The Brentanos' eldest son, John F. Theodore B. Brentano, was appointed as the first Postmaster of St. Paul when the Post Office was opened on June 24, 1874. He became a self-educated legal expert and won many cases before the bar, even though he was not a lawyer. On June 19, 1893, he was appointed Indian Agent for the Grande Ronde Indian Reservation by President Cleveland.

Dr. and Mrs. Brentano had three children, as follows: John F. Theodore Boniface, who married Kate Ahern, a native of County Cork, Ireland, who lived with her aunt in St. Paul; Ringner S. L. M., who married Mary Ernst of St. Paul; and Casimer, who married Dora Thoma of Dayton, Oregon.

Dr. John Brentano died at the age of 82 on February 10, 1902. Mrs. Brentano died on December 24, 1905, at the age of 87.

The Brentanos were happy and dependable, and they loved practical jokes. They were fervent members of the St. Paul Catholic Church. Over the years, many times when patients were unable to pay for their medical services Dr. Brentano forgave the financial obligation.

ALPHONSE J. BUYSERIE AND ISADORE F. BUYSERIE

Father DeFraine, Alphonse Buyserie, a friend of Father DeFraine and Isadore Buyserie

Agnes Buyserie McKay Collection

Alphonse J. Buyserie was born in 1870, and his brother Isadore F. Buyserie was born in 1872. They were the sons of Louis Buyserie and Sophie (DeFraine) Buyserie of Grammont, Belgium.

In 1884, the Buyserie brothers left Belgium and came to the United States. After spending a year in Lebanon, Kentucky, where their uncle, Father DeFraine, was stationed at the Trappist Abbey, they went to Seattle, Washington. From there they decided to go to the Benedictine Abbey in Mt. Angel, Oregon. When they arrived in Gervais on their way to Mt. Angel, they had only twenty-five cents between them. They bought sandwiches and a loaf of bread with the twenty-five cents and ate them on their walk to Mt. Angel. They were given jobs at the abbey and worked there for about a year. In 1886, James McKay of St. Paul offered them jobs at his flour mill and farm, where they worked for several years. By 1898, they had saved enough money to pur-

chase some timbered land about two and one-half miles
northeast of St. Paul. They cleared it and it became their
farm. In 1902, Isadore sold his interest in the farm to Alphonse and then purchased an adjoining tract of land.

Mary Berhorst was born October 2, 1868, in Missouri.
As a young girl she came to Oregon with the Kuensting
family. On February 2, 1891, she married Alphonse Buyserie. The couple were married in St. Paul by the Rev. F. X.
Blanchet.

Anna Hofer, the daughter of Mr. and Mrs. Hofer of
Champoeg, was born in 1879. On November 25, 1902, she
married Isadore Buyserie in St. Paul.

Alphonse Buyserie was 93 when he died on November 21,
1961. His wife Mary died at age 54 on February 15, 1922.

Isadore (Dory) Buyserie died on March 31, 1961, at age
91, and his wife Anna was 84 when she died on October
30, 1963.

The Buyseries were industrious, friendly and hardwork-
ing. Their integrity was unquestioned. They were excellent
farmers and raised fine herds of cattle in addition to grain,
corn and clover.

"China Pheasant Time" in St. Paul

Beverly Lambert Bush Collection

AMADEE E. CHOQUETTE AND MARIE (BERNIER) CHOQUETTE

The Amadee Choquette Family

Delight Lorenz Collection

Amadee Choquette was born about 1840 in St. Gregoire, Montreal, Canada. He was the son of Charles Choquette and Elinor (Seguin) Choquette. As a youth he studied for the priesthood, but eventually decided that he would rather go west. He arrived in St. Paul when a young man in his teens, and eventually purchased a farm about two and a half miles southeast of St. Paul.

Marie Bernier was born in St. Paul April 30, 1845. Her father, Francois Bernier, Jr., was the son of Francois Bernier and Genevieve (Layole) Bernier of Maskinonge, Canada, where Francois, Jr. had been born. After Francois Bernier, Jr. came to St. Paul he worked as a miller and had a farm. He went to California during the gold rush. Marie Bernier's mother was Pelagie Lucier, a daughter of Etienne Lucier and Josephite of the Nouete Indian tribe. Pelagie was born in 1826.

Etienne Lucier was a French Canadian who had come west with the Astor Expedition's Hunt Party in 1811 when he was 18 years old. His farm, about three and a half miles north of St. Paul, was one of the first farms in the Oregon Country. In late 1838, Etienne Lucier and his neighbor, Pierre Belleque, met Father Blanchet when he arrived at Fort Vancouver when he came to French Prairie to bless the mission church. Lucier and Belleque organized the notification to the French Canadians that Father Blanchet would be at the church on January 6, 1839. At the meeting in Champoeg on May 3, 1843, Etienne Lucier was one of the fifty-two who voted for the establishment of a provisional government.

Amadee Choquette, 19, and Marie Bernier, 14, were married in St. Louis, Oregon on July 25, 1859. The witnesses were Etienne Lucier; Julie Gervais; Andre Lachapelie, uncle of the bride; and Amadee Seguin, uncle of the bridegroom.

After the wedding the Choquettes lived on their farm. They had some of the first and finest farm machinery in the St. Paul area. They also bred trotting horses. Two of the best were "Emigrant" and "Champoeg". The Choquette farm was a very successful operation and eventually the Choquettes became relatively wealthy. Three of their daughters married sons of Honore (Henri) Picard of St. Paul. Celina Choquette married John Picard, who as a youth worked for the Jette store and in the harvests in eastern Oregon. He later built a home on his farm in St. Paul, had a ferry across the Willamette, and had the main blacksmith shop in St. Paul. One of John Picard's granddaughters, Delight (McHale) Lorenz, became an actress and has been prominent in theater circles in Portland for many years.

The Amadee Choquettes had 15 children, as follows: Mary, who married Henri Picard II; Celina, who married John Adolph Picard; Eleanor (Dolly), who married Jewell Picard; Delia, who married Joseph Delysle; Mamie, who married Chester Knight; Rose, who married Roger White; and Amadee, Fique, Theresa, Leo, Charles, George, Pierre, Felix and Freeman.

Amadee Choquette died at age 68 on October 7, 1908. Mrs. Choquette died when 47 years of age on June 16, 1892.

The Choquettes were a prominent early day St. Paul family. Their children, who were talented musicians, loved social affairs and were very happy people. They had a baseball diamond on their farm, and a piano from France was one of the family's prized possessions. Neighbors would gather at their farm in the evenings and on Sundays for athletic events, singing and dancing. The entire family had a great love for horses.

Amadee Choquette carried a scar on his arm. When he was coming across the plains he encountered a grizzly bear which chewed on his arm and then hid him by covering him with leaves. As soon as the bear was a safe distance away Mr. Choquette got up and left quickly so he wouldn't be there when the bear returned, but the bear had left its mark.

John Picard and his dog

Delight Lorenz Collection

Two St. Paul Postmasters
Peter McDonald and John F.T.B. Brentano

St. Paul Mission Historical Society

JAMES COLEMAN AND
FRANCES (MURRAY) COLEMAN

James Coleman
Mr. and Mrs. Frank Coleman

F. R. Coleman Collection

James Coleman was born in Franklin, Warren County, Ohio, on July 21, 1821. His father was born in Pennsylvania and his grandfather in Holland. By the time he was 13 the family had moved to Johnson County, Indiana, and James was supporting himself by working in a tan yard. When he was 18 he drove a team to Louisa County, Iowa. He liked

Iowa so well that he stayed and found work on the farms in the area.

Frances Murray was born in Ireland in 1824. When she was an infant she crossed the Atlantic with her father, Barney Murray. The Murrays settled in Iowa.

On June 5, 1845, James Coleman, 23, and Frances Murray, 21, were married in Iowa. The following year their daughter Anna was born.

In the spring of 1847, the Colemans outfitted themselves with a covered wagon, four yoke of oxen, necessary supplies and some stock which they planned to use in starting their farming operation in the Willamette Valley. Some of the cattle were appropriated by the Indians on the way. The train, which came by way of Fort Hall on the Snake River, was under the command of Captains Davidson and Mendenhall. In St. Paul, Mr. Coleman found an opportunity for a livelihood by working at the mission sawmill during the first winter. During the spring of 1848, he took up a donation land claim near Little Muddy Creek, seven miles north of present day McMinnville in Yamhill County, adjacent to the claim of his friend Miles McDonald. He built a log house, which was to be the family home for twelve years.

In the spring of 1849, after leaving his wife and small daughter at the St. Paul Mission, Mr. Coleman went to the California gold fields by pack horse. He mined on the American River for six weeks and later tried his luck on Angel Creek. After clearing about a thousand dollars he returned to St. Paul late in the year. Then he and his wife and daughter returned to the donation land claim in Yamhill County. In 1860, Mr. Coleman sold that claim and came to St. Paul, where he purchased 320 acres. He never occupied the land, but hired a manager to run it as a cattle ranch. In the fall of 1862, he sold the 320 acres and purchased 900 acres of the Sauvie and Lambert land claims about a mile south of St. Paul. He built a large home on this property and successfully farmed the land for about 30 years.

Mr. and Mrs. James Coleman had eleven children, as follows: Anna, who married W. F. Davidson of St. Paul;

John, who married Mary Kennedy of St. Paul; Mary Eliza-
beth, who married Charles O. Pelland of St. Paul; James
R., who married Eliza Miller of Salem; William Thomas,
who married Caledonia Orton of Yamhill County; Eliza-
beth, who married F. C. Hammond of Juneau, Alaska;
Stephen, who married Dorothy Turner of Portland; Charles
D., who remained single; Emily, who married William
Murphy of St. Paul; Helen, who married John Casey of
Portland; and Frank N., who married Mary Ellen Jackson
of Hubbard, Oregon.

Mrs. Frances Coleman died at 72 years of age on April
25, 1896. James Coleman died when 89 years of age on
June 11, 1911.

The Coleman children were all well educated. The girls
attended St. Mary's Academy in Portland. All the sons except Frank attended Willamette University. Frank started
at Mt. Angel College when it opened in 1887 and graduated
from there in 1890. The Colemans were public-spirited
people who were always interested in improving the community. They became involved in all the social affairs and,
together with the other residents of St. Paul, would take
their turn hosting parties and furnishing the hay wagon
which was used to pick up the young people and take them
to and from the dances and parties in the community. The
Coleman family loved sports, particularly baseball, and
were enthusiastic participants. One of James Coleman's
grandsons, Curtis Coleman, was the third baseman for
the New York Highlanders—who became the New York
Yankees—in 1912. Mr. and Mrs. James Coleman, who lived
to celebrate their fiftieth wedding anniversary in 1895, and
their family contributed greatly to the social and cultural
life in St. Paul and were highly respected in the community.

MATTHEW CONNOR AND
MARY (LYNCH) CONNOR

The Matthew Connor Family

Gerald Connor Family Collection

Matthew Connor was born in 1823, in Killican, County Westmeath, Ireland. Mary Lynch was born in Reharney, County Westmeath. About 1845, Matthew Connor and Mary Lynch were married in Ireland.

Shortly after their marriage the Connors came to the United States and settled in St. Mary's, Minnesota, which is near Waseka, Minnesota. They purchased a farm there and became very close friends of the Peter Kirk and Andrew Hughes families, who were their neighbors. In 1870, the Kirks came to St. Paul and purchased a farm. Shortly thereafter Mr. Kirk purchased the Jesuit Mission property for his friends, the Connors. Mr. Connor had been wanting to move to a more temperate climate because of failing health. In 1871, the Connors, with their eight children, came to Oregon on the new transcontinental railroad. The Connors were happy with their new home because it was near a Catholic church, there were Catholic schools for the education of their children, and the land was much superior to that which they had farmed in Minnesota.

In 1875, four years after they arrived in St. Paul, Matthew Connor died. His family continued to operate the farm and Mission Landing, which was on their property. The landing was also known as St. Paul Landing. One of the Connor sons, Simon, was in charge of all wharfage there. He was also agent for the shipping company. Many steamboat passengers and people waiting for shipments would await the arrival of the steamboats at Simon Connor's home on the bluff overlooking the river. The boat captains knew this and always gave a toot well in advance so the waiting people would have plenty of time to finish their coffee and get down to the dock before the steamboat arrived. The typical passenger trip to Portland took three days—one day going, one day shopping and one day returning.

Mr. and Mrs. Matthew Connor had nine children, as follows: Matthew, who remained single; Simon, who married Agnes Scully of St. Paul, Minnesota; Thomas, who married Catherine McGrath of St. Paul; Lucy, who married John E. Kennedy of St. Paul; Jane, who remained single; Anne, who became Sr. Mary Bridget of the Holy Names Sisters; Bridget, who became Sr. Mary Eva of the Holy Names Sisters; Rose, who married Andrew Hughes of St. Paul; and Martha, who died when a young girl.

Mrs. Mary (Lynch) Connor died when 84 years of age in 1906.

The Connors were friendly people who had a fine sense of humor. They were hard working and morally strong. They were very religious and were very involved with the church, which was intricately interwoven with the religious and social life in St. Paul. It was said of Mrs. Connor that in her later years she knew only one path, and that was to the church where she went almost daily for Mass.

JOHN J. COOKE AND
BRIDGET (LEE) COOKE

Mr. and Mrs. John Cooke

Jean Abner Collection

John J. Cooke was born June 24, 1829, in County Limerick, Ireland. He and his brother Nicholas were sons of Patrick Cooke and Susanne (Calahan) Cooke. In 1845, at age 16, John Cooke stowed away on a ship bound for New York because he did not want to be conscripted by the British Army. He had only a small amount of money when he arrived in New York. After working in New York for a short while he decided to go to the Oregon Country. In Indiana, where he met some people who were preparing to cross the plains, John agreed to drive cattle for them in return for board and lodging; and the group left for Oregon via the Applegate Trail.

John Cooke arrived in St. Paul in early 1846. In 1847, he joined the Oregon Volunteers and fought in the Cayuse Indian War as a private in Company D, 5th Regiment, Oregon Army. After the war he went to southern Oregon and panned for gold. In September 1853, he took up a donation land claim near Ashland in Jackson County. He wrote to his brother Nick in Ireland explaining that he could file a land claim if he was in Oregon.

Mrs. Cooke died after John's emigration and eventually his father and brother left Ireland for the Oregon Territory. Mr. Cooke died on the way in Illinois and Nick subsequently obtained a job driving cattle to Oregon. When he arrived in Oregon he didn't know where his brother lived, but he happened to meet a man who told him there was a John Cooke living near Ashland. Nick went there, found his brother, and took up a land claim near Ashland.

In early 1858, John Cooke returned to St. Paul after a ten-year absence. He purchased the Dr. James Scheil donation land claim about one mile east of St. Paul.

Bridget Lee was born April 11, 1831, in Tyrellspass, County Westmeath, Ireland. She was the daughter of Patrick Lee and Mary (Burns) Lee. Patrick Lee was a second cousin of General Robert E. Lee of Civil War fame. Mary (Burns) Lee was the sister of Hugh Burns, who came to Oregon in 1842, and Ellen (Burns) Gearin of St. Paul.

In 1855, Bridget Lee left Ireland with several of her cousins and came to Oregon by steamship via Cape Horn and San Francisco. After she arrived she stayed with her aunt, Mrs. Gearin, and her uncle, Hugh Burns, who had a log cabin on his claim near Oregon City. At the time Oregon City had a reputation for roughness, with many Indians, trappers, gamblers, saloon girls and former Hudson's Bay Company men living there.

On September 11, 1860, John Cooke, 31, and Bridget Lee, 29, were married in the St. Paul Catholic Church.

After the wedding the couple lived in a log cabin on their farm. In addition to operating the farm, Mr. Cooke conducted land surveys in the St. Paul area. He was clerk of the St. Paul Public School from 1861 until 1869. Charles Ray, who had the Oregon City-Salem mail route and stage-coaches, said that he was always happy to arrive at the Cookes' place as Bridget Cooke would always wave to him as he passed. Three of Bridget Cooke's brothers came to Oregon, but they all returned to Ireland prior to 1870.

The Cookes replaced the log cabin with a small one-story house, and then in 1882 they built a two-story house. It was one of the first houses in the St. Paul area to contain indoor plumbing. The two eldest Cooke sons, Jim and Nick, were among the students in attendance when Four Corners Public School opened in 1874.

Mr. and Mrs. John Cooke had six children. They were: Nicholas, who married E. Mietz of Germany; James Lee, who married Agnes Bunnenmeyer of Xenia, Ohio; Robert, who married Sarah Grey; Mary, who remained single; John J.; and Joseph, who married M. Hewett.

John J. Cooke died at age 53 on December 31, 1882. Bridget (Lee) Cooke lived until March 22, 1908. She was 76 when she died.

The Cookes were greatly interested in all community activities. Mr. Cooke kept a surveyor's notebook which tells much about early day St. Paul. Bridget Lee's uncle, Hugh Burns, was a frequent visitor at their farm. In a letter written in Ireland in 1892, James Martin, Sr., a cousin of Mrs. James McKay who had visited in St. Paul, said of Mrs. Cooke, ". . . She was always very kind to me whenever I called and if she were nearer I would gladly send her a bottle of genuine 'poteen' as a remembrance of the many pleasant social visits I made at her mansion. . ." The Cookes were very friendly people, and everybody enjoyed visiting with them.

Goats returning from pasture
(Northern view from near the center of St. Paul—1895)

Gerald Connor Family Collection

HUGH COSGROVE AND
MARY (ROSITER) COSGROVE

Mr. and Mrs. Hugh Cosgrove

Ardis LeFebvre Collection

Hugh Cosgrove was born in Ulster, Northern Ireland, on December 24, 1802. His father was a farmer, who in 1808 decided to take advantage of the opportunities he had heard about in Canada. The Cosgroves came to Canada and took up a 100 acre wooded tract of land near Lanark in lower Canada, where Hugh spent his boyhood going to school and helping clear the land of its hardwood timber.

Mary Rositer was born in County Wexford, Ireland, on May 3, 1811. Her father, Richard Rositer, came to Canada with his family and settled in Perth.

In 1825, Hugh Cosgrove, 23, and Mary Rositer, 14, were married in Perth.

The couple moved west and settled in Chatham, Canada, where they took up a 200 acre farm. In 1830, when it appeared that there might be a war between the Canadians and the Americans, the Cosgroves moved to Detroit. While there they purchased cows in Canada for $10 a head and sold them in Michigan for as much as $40. Mr. Cosgrove later obtained a contract for grading the new railroad between Chicago and Detroit and made $5,000 from the venture. In 1832, the couple moved to Illinois. Mr. Cosgrove took a contract for excavating and filling on the canal from Chicago to the Mississippi River. The Cosgroves then moved to Joliet, Illinois, where they purchased a 160 acre farm. In 1846, because of malaria on the Illinois prairie and because of favorable accounts about the Oregon Country in the Joplin newspaper, the *Courier*, the Cosgroves decided to cross the plains to the Willamette Valley.

In early 1847, a party of 13 families from Joliet, including Lot Whitcomb of later Oregon steamboat fame, the Hugh Cosgroves, the James McKays, and John Hunt left Joliet by wagon train. The Cosgroves, who were quite well off because of their successful ventures, had three wagons, each drawn by three yoke of young oxen, and 15 cows. The wagon train party drove across Illinois, Iowa and Missouri in the springtime when the grass was beginning to grow. At St. Joseph, Missouri they waited their turn for about a week to cross the Missouri River. They then continued west. Indians of many tribes followed the wagon train, and they were given a little sugar or tobacco. Once about 40 Pawnee Indians tried to stampede the train, but gave up after a short while. The first wild animals encountered were antelope, which Mr. Cosgrove's large greyhounds were able to overtake. Wolves were the most frequent visitors, and coyotes yelped at nearly every campfire. For some time the travellers saw many buffalo chips, which were used for campfire, but no buffalo. Then one morning in the Platte River Valley they encountered a herd estimated at 100,000, which took four hours to thunder past the wagons after having been split by riders on horseback. One buffalo, which was shot when running toward the train, weighed about 2,200 pounds. From there until the Continental Divide buffalo was the main wild meat. Birds were abundant and rattlesnakes were innumerable. West of the Continental Divide salmon was the main wild food. It was easy to obtain from Indians in exchange for a trinket.

After crossing the Blue Mountains in eastern Oregon, the party met Dr. and Mrs. Marcus Whitman and Dr. and Mrs. Spaulding. Dr. Whitman gave Mr. Cosgrove, who had been quite ill, some fresh fruit; and traded him a horse for a cow which had become foot sore. At The Dalles Mr. Cosgrove hired a boat and made a comfortable voyage down the Columbia River. On arriving at Vancouver he rented a house and left his family there while he looked over the country. Mr. Peter Skeene Ogden, the governor at Fort Vancouver, advised him to go up the Willamette Valley if he wanted to farm. He went to the St. Paul area and purchased a 320 acre section of land adjoining the mission for $800, two oxen and two cows. The land contained a fairly good house. Cosgrove planted 40 acres of wheat that fall after preparing the ground with sod plows he brought with him. When the Cosgroves went to their first social meeting in St. Paul they found that the swallowtail coats, high silk hats and fancy dresses and bonnets which they were wearing created quite a surprise to the local population; there the men sat on one side of the room, and the women, wearing red handkerchiefs for head covering, sat on the other. Soon Mrs. Cosgrove was teaching the women how to weave wheat straw and make chip hats and bonnets; but the men had no desire for swallowtail coats and silk hats.

In the spring of 1848, Mr. Cosgrove left for the gold fields in California. After being fairly successful in the mines he returned to St. Paul in December 1848. He put his six daughters in the Sisters of Notre Dame School in Oregon City. Then in the spring of 1849, Mr. and Mrs. Cosgrove and their two sons left for California. After stopping for a while at Jacksonville, they proceeded to Placerville, California. They established a store there. They made $15,000 in twenty months and then purchased about $15,000 worth of goods in San Francisco, which they brought back to St. Paul by steamboat and riverboat. They had been gone so long that the youngest daughter, Caroline, did not at first recognize her father and mother.

They opened a store on their property and operated it for about six years. After 1857, the Cosgroves just operated their farm, as Mr. Cosgrove preferred farming to merchandising. From the time the Cosgroves first arrived in St. Paul, their house was a sort of unofficial home for the travelling public. Among the many guests was Aaron Meier, a peddler, who travelled on foot and would stay overnight without charge. He later had a store at Champoeg and eventually started the Meier and Frank store in Portland.

The Cosgroves had ten children. They were: Marguerite, who married Theodore Poujade, son of a prominent St. Louis, Oregon doctor who had come from France; Anna, who married Freeman Eldridge of Fairfield, who had purchased the Joseph Gervais claim and later the Xavier Ladieroute claim and eventually produced 40,000 bushels of grain annually from his 2,000 acres; Mary, Anna's twin, who married James Costello, the postmaster at Champoeg, and later after Mr. Costello died, Jerome Jackson (Jerome Jackson was a cousin of President Andrew Jackson who had come from Booneville, New York to Oregon in 1839 via Cape Horn when he was 15 years old. He lived on his 420 acre land claim which he had taken up in 1839.); Elizabeth, a twin to a boy who had died in childhood, who married Andrew Murphy, who had a farm adjoining the Cosgroves; James, who died when 23 years of age; Susan, who remained single; Caroline, who married W. D. Vantine of New York City; Hugh, who married Emma (Stanley) Clifton of Albany, Oregon; and Emeline, who married D. F. Wagner, who was the agent for the Wells Fargo Express Company at Idaho City, Idaho, and later at Salem.

Mary (Rositer) Cosgrove died in St. Paul on September 15, 1872, at age 62. Hugh Cosgrove died in St. Paul when he was 98 years of age on April 10, 1901.

The Cosgroves were a key family in the development of St. Paul. They were enterprising, hospitable and always interested in improving the community. They were among the leaders in the social life, and their integrity was unquestioned. Mrs. Cosgrove was a leader in helping organize church affairs and was godmother for many of the early immigrant children baptized in St. Paul. Mr. Cosgrove's sense of humor brought laughter and light-heartedness to the thriving community.

WILLIAM FRANKLIN DAVIDSON AND ANNA (COLEMAN) DAVIDSON

Mr. and Mrs. William Franklin Davidson

Alice Davidson Collection

William Franklin Davidson was born March 28, 1843, in Stark County, Illinois. His parents were Green Clay Davidson and Nancy (Million) Davidson. Green Clay's father, who was born in England, served as a Captain in the U.S. Army in the War of 1812. Nancy Million descended from an old Virginia family and was born in Kentucky, where her parents were extensive cotton planters and slave owners. Green Clay Davidson was a juggler for the Sands and Lee Circus, and met Nancy Million while on tour with the circus in Kentucky.

After the couple were married, Green Clay was injured while performing a hangman's act for the circus and had to use a silver breathing tube for three months. He then decided to change occupations, and the couple took up a 160 acre homestead in Stark County, Illinois, where they stayed for four years. While there William Franklin was born. The Davidsons then moved to Peoria, Illinois, where they purchased a hotel and livery barn.

On March 28, 1852, the family set out for Oregon, crossing the plains by horse-drawn covered wagon in a party of 250. Their son William Franklin was nine years old at the time. After stopping for a short while at Forest Grove, Oregon, they moved to Dayton in early 1853, and purchased another hotel and livery stable. The business was very successful, and after two years they purchased a half interest in a mercantile store. They continued to prosper the next two years. In 1857, they disposed of the enterprises and moved to St. Paul, where they purchased the 640 acre Deguire land claim and ferry. They operated the ferry and built a store and warehouse. In the bad flood of 1861, Mr. Davidson lost 20,000 bushels of grain—mostly wheat and oats—worth $2 a bushel. The loss was so great that he was eventually forced to sell everything he had to pay his creditors. Then, starting from practically nothing, he managed to establish a store in Fairfield. After operating the store for three years the Green Clay Davidsons moved to Salem.

Anna Coleman, the eldest daughter of the James Colemans of St. Paul, was born in Louisa County, Iowa, and crossed the plains to Oregon in a covered wagon when she was one year old. She was the first daughter of American immigrants to be baptized in the brick church. She lived with her parents in Yamhill County until the family moved to St. Paul when she was 16 years old.

On May 24, 1864, William Franklin Davidson, 22, and Anna Coleman, 19, were married in the St. Paul Catholic Church.

The young couple first rented land from Mrs. Davidson's father and farmed for several years. They later operated a sawmill near Fairfield. In 1867, they purchased 320 acres about one and a half miles southeast of St. Paul, and began a farming operation which was to be carried on successfully for many years. They raised wheat, oats, corn and clover and had horses, cattle and hogs. As time went on they added rather large hop fields to their general farming operations. For thirty years, including ten years as Roads Commissioner, Mr. Davidson contributed greatly to the development of better roads in the area.

The Davidsons' sons, James "Fred", Eugene "Gene", John "Jack", and Ralph, conducted large and very successful farming operations in the St. Paul area for many years. Chester, the youngest son, was one of the better carpenters in the community. As they were growing up they were interested in all types of sports and had a race track adjacent to their farm. Each Sunday many of the St. Paul residents would gather there for horse races. The Davidson boys were among the best jockeys in the community. One, John "Jack", was one of the fastest foot racers in St. Paul. James "Fred" Davidson's son, Harold Davidson, served as Portland City Attorney from 1933 to 1942. Harold's sister Alice, who was a member of St. Paul High School's first graduating class, began a long and distinguished teaching career at Four Corners Public School in the early 1920's.

Mr. and Mrs. W. F. Davidson had twelve children, as follows: Mary, who married Hugh Kirkpatrick of Idaho; Laura, who married Jerome Jackson of Hubbard; Jane, who married James Smith of St. Paul; Arzelia, who married Paul Reedie of Salem; James "Fred", who married Mary Anna Gooding of St. Paul; John "Jack", who married Clara Merten of St. Paul; Blanche, who married Charles Gooding of St. Paul; Edna, who died in early childhood; Eugene, who married Elizabeth Merten of St. Paul; Ralph, who married Hazel Littlefield of Newberg; Hilda, who married Fred Gearin of St. Paul; and Chester, who married Gretchen Breyman.

On April 24, 1907, Mrs. Davidson died at age 61. Mr. Davidson died on February 13, 1927, when he was 84.

Mr. and Mrs. W. F. Davidson and their children were friendly, hard working, good conversationalists, and active participants in the social affairs of the area. They and their descendants have been a vital part of the St. Paul community for about 120 years. At the present time the fifth generation of Davidsons, whose original St. Paul ancestors were the Green Clay Davidsons and the James Colemans, are operating some of the most productive farms in the St. Paul area.

FRANCOIS HENRY ERNST AND MARY MADELINE (VESER) ERNST

Mr. and Mrs. Francois Ernst

Norman Ernst Collection

Francois Ernst was born in Colmar, Alsace, France, on July 3, 1840. His father served in the French Army under Napoleon I and participated in the Battle of Waterloo. Francois Ernst served in the French Army under Napoleon III.

Mary Madeline Veser was born October 2, 1838, in Colmar. In 1865, Francois Ernst, 25, and Mary Madeline Veser, 27, were married.

The following year their first child, Mary, was born in Paris. In 1869, the Ernsts decided to come to the United States. After arriving in New York they went to San Francisco by steamship, crossing the Isthmus of Panama by railroad. They proceeded up the coast by steamship and finally arrived at Westminster, British Columbia, via the Frazier River. They then travelled to Hope, British Columbia and settled near Mr. Ernst's sister, Ann, who had come there earlier. While there a son, Henry, was born to the Ernsts in 1870. In 1871, they left Hope by mule train and crossed the mountains to Colville, Washington, where a second son, Louis, was born on Christmas Eve, 1871. In 1872, they went by mule train to The Dalles, Oregon, and then by boat to Portland. For about a year they stayed in Portland, where Mr. Ernst obtained a job as a shoemaker. He walked six miles to and from work each day. While there he heard that St. Paul needed a shoemaker.

He went to St. Paul and found that they did indeed need a shoemaker. He was told further that if, in addition to being a shoemaker, he would ring the "Angelus" three times a day, he would be given three acres of land. So, in 1873, the Ernsts moved to St. Paul. They lived in a log house, and Mr. Ernst operated the shoe shop and rang the "Angelus". He worked hard; and even though times were difficult, he managed to make enough to sustain his growing family. In the late 1870's, business boomed because of all the men who were in the St. Paul area building the railroad. On October 4, 1880, when the narrow gauge railroad from St. Paul to Silverton was completed, the railroad company invited the St. Paul citizens to ride on the first trip to Silverton. The Ernst boys, ten-year old Henry and eight-year old Louis, along with the other St. Paul boys, carried buckets of rocks and had a contest to see who could hit the most telegraph poles from the moving flat car. A tragedy struck the Ernst family in 1883 when their sons, Paul, 9, and Alphonse, 4, died from diphtheria within four days of one another.

As time went on the profits from the shoe shop increased and the Ernsts were able to live reasonably well. Henry and Louis established a successful logging operation near Harrisburg, Oregon. They brought the logs by raft to the lower Willamette Valley mills and made enough money to buy property in the St. Paul area. Henry Ernst established Ernst's Hardware Store in St. Paul, and during the Great Depression many of the farmers in the St. Paul area had rather large credit accounts with him. He had a reputation for being lenient with those who owed him money, and in spite of this he was generally among the first to be paid when an individual had enough money to pay some bills. Practically everybody eventually paid him in full for everything they had purchased on credit at his store. His brother Louis had a farm, which contained the St. Paul peach orchard, about one and a half miles west of St. Paul. Louis' son Norman was an accomplished piano player and played for the St. Paul dances for about 40 years. Phillipina Ernst married Barney Krechter, who owned one of the saloons in St. Paul; and their son Joseph became a nationally known musician. He played for Paramount Pictures, became a member of Paul Whiteman's Band, and arranged music for Bing Crosby. Anthime "Tim", who was also a talented musician, settled in Silverdale, Washington and operated a meat market there.

The Francois Ernsts had seven children, as follows: Mary, who married Ringner Brentano of St. Paul; Henry, who married Dorothy Eder of St. Paul; Louis, who married Mary Thoma of Dayton, Oregon; Anthime "Tim", who married Grace Dee Miller of Illinois; Phillipina, who married Bernard Krechter of St. Paul; and Paul and Alphonse, who died when young boys.

Mrs. Ernst died at 78 years of age on June 26, 1917. Francois Ernst died on August 22, 1926, when 86.

The Ernst family was hard working, industrious, deeply religious and highly respected in the community. The boys served Mass for Archbishop Blanchet when they were young, and later were among the better baseball players in the community. Mrs. Ernst walked the mile and a half from her home to the church for Mass, even in her later years.

JOHN GEARIN AND
ELLEN (BURNS) GEARIN

John M. Gearin
Mr. and Mrs. Hugh Gearin

Tim Gearin Collection

John Gearin, son of Cornelius Gearin and Ellen (Cavanaugh) Gearin, was born in 1808 in Dingle, County Kerry, Ireland. As a youth he learned the shoemaker trade and was employed in that trade in Ireland, where he married Catherine Thourow before he and his wife and small children came to Boston in 1834. While there John Gearin worked in the shipyards and on the docks. Eventually he and his family moved to Fort Wayne, Indiana, where they purchased a farm. Shortly after moving to Fort Wayne, Mrs. Gearin died. Great adjustments were necessary, but Mr. Gearin and his three young children continued to operate the farm.

Ellen Burns, born in 1807, was the third of eight children born to the John Burns family of Tyrellspass, County Westmeath, Ireland. Her eldest brother, James, came to America and became a ship's captain sailing out of Boston. He sent for Ellen, but when she arrived in Baltimore about 1830 she found that her brother's ship had been captured by the notorious pirate "Gibbs" and that her brother had been killed in the course of the incident. She found employment with the wife of an army officer, and about a year later married John Costello, whom she had met on the ship coming to America. After living in Baltimore for several years the Costellos decided to move to Fort Wayne, Indiana. At the time they had two children. In Fort Wayne they operated a hotel in the Old Council House, where the Territorial Governor had previously met with the leaders of the various Indian tribes. Mr. Costello also trucked supplies to Michigan by wagon. He later purchased two tracts of timbered land which he partially cleared and then farmed. In 1847, Mr. Costello died, leaving Mrs. Costello with a partially cleared farm and five young children.

In early 1849, John Gearin, 40, and Ellen Costello, 41, were married in Fort Wayne. In the spring of that year Mrs. Gearin's eldest son, James Costello, left for the gold fields. The Gearins operated their combined farm and a son, Hugh Burns Gearin, was born on October 9, 1849. Mrs. Gearin began to receive glowing reports of the Oregon Country from her younger brother Hugh Burns, who had come to Oregon in 1842 with the first organized wagon train to cross the great plains, and had been one of the leaders in setting up the meeting at Champoeg which established a Provisional Government on May 2, 1843. Because of these reports of Oregon from her brother Hugh and another brother, Lawrence, who was also in Oregon, the Gearins decided to come west. In early 1851, the Gearins arranged for the combined farm to be operated by Mr. Gearin's eldest son, Cornelius, and started making plans to go west.

Their party consisted of Mr. and Mrs. Gearin, Ellen Gearin, Mary Ellen Costello, John Costello, Michael Costello and young Hugh Gearin. They had a covered wagon, six yoke of oxen, five cows, a riding pony, and necessary supplies. They joined a party of about twenty-five other families who were among the throng of families going west. As they neared their destination, about five months after they started the journey, on August 15, 1851, another son, John McDermott Gearin, was born near the bank of the Umatilla River. After they arrived in St. Paul in the fall of 1851, the Gearins paid $500 for 320 acres of heavily timbered land about three miles north of St. Paul. The sellers were named Guardupuis. The land was part of the Belleque Donation Land Claim. The family immediately started building a small log house and clearing some additional land.

The Gearins' farm thrived and eventually it expanded to 1,600 acres and extended to the bank of the Willamette River. It had grain fields, hop yards, apple orchards and many farm animals. The Gearins established Gearin's Ferry and Landing for shipping produce up and down the Willamette River and across the river to Dayton.

They moved from the small log house to a small board house and eventually, in about 1875, to a large two-story house containing two library-parlors, two living rooms, two fireplaces, two dining rooms, two kitchens, six bedrooms, two bathrooms and a 30 by 60 foot recreation room. The large home became one of the centers of social activity in the St. Paul area.

Their son Hugh was educated in the Catholic Seminary in Oregon City and the second son, John, graduated from Notre Dame University. Hugh assisted his father with the operation of the farm, and about 1890 joined an expedition to Alaska and Siberia which included Governor Lane's son and friends of Theodore Roosevelt. John served in the Oregon Legislature and eventually became United States Senator from Oregon. He came to be known as a "silver-tongued orator".

Mr. and Mrs. John Gearin, Sr. had two children. Hugh married Mary Cecelia (Minnie) Murphy of St. Paul, and John married Matilda Raleigh of Yamhill County. Mr. Gearin's daughter Ellen, by his previous marriage, married Charles Marks of Fort Wayne. Mrs. Gearin's children by her former marriage who came to Oregon were: James, who married Mary Cosgrove of St. Paul; Mary Ellen, who married Matthew Murphy of St. Paul; John; and Michael, who died in his late teens.

Mrs. Ellen (Burns) Gearin died in 1879, at 72 years of age. John Gearin died when 85 in 1893.

The Gearins were adventurous, enterprising and morally strong. They valued education and were not only very successful farmers, but were leaders in the social life of the community. They loved to have a house full of happy people.

Two St. Paul natives—John Gearin and a bear. The bear was one of two cubs which were found in a timbered area near St. Paul in the late 1890's and raised by the Gearins. They were kept in two large cages in front of the Gearin home.

Dr. John Gearin Collection

NICHOLAS GOODING AND
MARY (ERBSLAND) GOODING

The Nicholas Gooding Family

Elmer Gooding Collection

Nicholas Gooding was born in Alsace-Lorraine on January 18, 1832. When he was twelve years old he came to the United States with his parents, who settled near St. Ann's, Indiana. The family farmed and operated a sawmill and Nicholas served an apprenticeship with a blacksmith. In 1849, when he was 17 years of age, he opened a blacksmith shop of his own. After operating the blacksmith shop for twelve years he had saved enough money to purchase a farm near Mt. Vernon, Indiana.

On August 28, 1860, Nicholas Gooding, 28, and Mary Erbsland, 21, daughter of Joseph and Tracy (Lang) Erbsland, were married in St. Ann's.

After operating the farm for 28 years, the Goodings contemplated moving to Oregon. Nicholas Gooding and one of his sons, George, came to Oregon in 1888 to get an idea of conditions there. George stayed in Butteville and Mr. Gooding returned to Indiana. The next year Mr. Gooding, with his sons Charles and John, returned to Oregon by rail. They brought a sawmill and horse-drawn steam propelled threshing machine with them. As they had heard about "the river bend on French Prairie" they came to St. Paul to look over the area. They purchased a 75 acre farm known as the Gratton Farm about two and a half miles southeast of St. Paul and set up a sawmill nearby.

The next year, 1890, Mrs. Gooding and the remainder of the family left Mt. Vernon, Indiana, and came to St. Paul. Nicholas Gooding's sister Theresa, who had married Stephen Merten in Minnesota and had been living in Nevada, came to St. Paul in 1889.

The Goodings operated their sawmill and had a commercial threshing machine business, in addition to operating the farm. Many of the older present day St. Paul homes were built from lumber produced by the Goodings, and their threshing machine business continued for more than forty years. In 1895, Nicholas Gooding purchased the 171 acre Clary farm about three-quarters of a mile east of St. Paul. He established a blacksmith shop on the farm, and soon everybody was saying that he "could make anything from iron".

John Gooding, who supervised the threshing machine business, was one of the first to grow strawberries commercially in the St. Paul area. One of Charles Gooding's sons, Bertrand "Bert", was an outstanding football player at the University of Oregon, where he obtained his law degree. He was a prominent attorney in Portland for many years and was active in Republican Party circles in Oregon. Several of Mr. and Mrs. Nicholas Gooding's sons were members of the St. Paul band, which was reputed to have been one of the best bands in Marion County.

Mr. and Mrs. Gooding had twelve children. They were: George, who married Sarah Keil of Aurora; Elizabeth, who married John Glatt of Jennings County, Indiana; John and Theresa, who remained single; Charles, who married Blanche Davidson of St. Paul; Lawrence, who married Emma Waltz of St. Paul; Joseph, who married Rose Dietrich; Anne, who married James "Fred" Davidson of St. Paul; and William, who married Matilda Waltz of

St. Paul. Three children, Tracy and twins Peter and Jacob, died in infancy.

Nicholas Gooding died at 78 years of age on November 4, 1910. Mrs. Gooding died at age 82 on February 23, 1922.

The Gooding family took an active part in everything that would benefit the community. They were expert mechanics. They were friendly, hard working, had a good sense of humor and were very close to the Church. Mrs. Gooding was accomplished at embroidery and made many of the altar cloths used in the St. Paul Church. One of the sons, William, was the church organist for many years.

ANDREW HUGHES AND ROSE (CONNOR) HUGHES

The Andrew Hughes Family

Elmer Hughes Collection

Andrew Hughes was born in County Meath, Ireland, in 1844. He was the son of Mr. and Mrs. Thomas Hughes of Rathcore, County Meath. The Hughes family left Ireland in 1848 at the time of the famine.

After coming to America the family settled on a farm near Waseka, Minnesota. As Andrew was growing up he worked on the farm, and did carpentry work on the side.

Rose Connor was born in Freeport, Illinois, on June 15, 1851. She had a twin brother, Simon. Her parents were Mr. and Mrs. Matthew Connor, natives of County Westmeath, Ireland.

Andrew Hughes and Rose Connor were married in the township of St. Mary's, Minnesota, in 1872.

After the couple were married they operated a small farm near Waseka. In 1874, when their eldest son Thomas was a baby, they left St. Cloud, Minnesota, and crossed the plains by covered wagon. They came to St. Paul, where Mrs. Hughes' father, Matthew Connor, had a farm. After they arrived they purchased a small farm adjacent to the Connor farm. In addition to operating the farm, Mr. Hughes did carpentry work, including the building of coffins. They continued to successfully operate the farm for many years.

Thomas Hughes' eldest son Elmer was in the first graduating class at St. Paul High School in 1923. Elmer and his brothers worked for the Crown Zellerbach paper mills at Calama, Washington; and Elmer eventually became Vice President in charge of production for Crown Zellerbach Corporation in San Francisco.

Mr. and Mrs. Andrew Hughes had ten children, as follows: Thomas, who married Magdalena "Lena" Krechter of St. Paul; Mary Ann, who married Peter Smith of St. Paul; Martha Jane "Jennie", who married Philip Mullen of St. Paul; Rose, who married Irwin McDowell of Portland; Evelyn "Eva", who married Webster Pillette of St. Paul; Agnes, who married Robert Faber of St. Paul; Angela, who married Stephen Merten of St. Paul; John, who married Mary McClosky of Portland; Lucy, who remained single; and Bertha, who died when seventeen years of age.

Andrew Hughes' sister Mary, who came from Ireland with the Thomas Hughes family, married John McGrath of St. Paul. One of Andrew's brothers went to Salinas, California, where he became a harness and saddlery merchant.

Andrew Hughes died at 72 years of age in 1916. Mrs. Hughes died in 1937 at the age of 86.

The Hughes family was hard working, congenial, vivacious and deeply religious. They participated enthusiastically in the social and religious affairs of the community.

ADOLPH JETTE AND
MARGUERITE (LIARD) JETTE

The Adolph Jette Family

Frank Jette Collection

Adolph Jette was born June 10, 1825, in Repentigny, Canada. His parents were Francois and Marie (Payette) Jette. Adolph Jette's first cousin, Louis Amable Jette, was the governor of Quebec and was a member of the committee of five which settled the Alaskan boundary question. For this he was made a Knight Bachelor by the King of England.

Adolph Jette came to the United States, lived in New York and later worked in sawmills in New Orleans, St. Louis and Fort Leavenworth, Kansas. While in Fort Leavenworth he was engaged by the United States government to drive supplies by ox team to Fort Laramie. In Fort Laramie he purchased an ox team and with several friends came to Canyon City, Oregon, where he mined for gold until 1856.

While there the miners encountered serious difficulties with the native tribes, eventually being surrounded for thirty days at the mouth of the Rogue River. Some miners lost their lives, but Mr. Jette was saved through the intercession of Chetsy, the daughter of a chief. He then went to Crescent City, California for a year and made a few hundred dollars.

In 1857, he decided to come to French Prairie with four friends from Canada whom he had met at Crescent City. On the trip north one night a young Indian girl came to where the party was camped and told them that the Indians were going to take their gold and kill them the next morning. She helped them escape and came with them to French Prairie. When they arrived they stayed at Louis Pichet's Log Inn at St. Paul. Mr. Pichet tried to place the young girl, Julie, with a native tribe, but none would take her; and four years later Mr. Pichet decided that one of the ones she had saved would have to marry her. All five drew straws and Mr. Jette, who drew the longest straw, married her. Mr. Jette had purchased a log house and lot in St. Paul in 1858, but for the following two years most of his time was spent in the mines in Idaho. In 1860, he went to work for the Davidson Store and Warehouse. In 1861, he married Julie, the Indian woman who had saved his life. After the 1861 flood washed away the Davidson Store and Warehouse, he became a clerk at the Haler Warehouse in Fairfield. In 1868,he went to work as a clerk for the Pelland-Larocque Store and Warehouse near Champoeg. Julie Jette died of consumption in 1865, and both daughters of the Jettes died in their early teens.

Marguerite Liard was born in St. Paul, on January 2, 1851. She was the daughter of Thomas and Celeste (Rocbrune) Liard. Her father was a French Canadian and her mother was a native of St. Paul whose father, Joseph Rocbrune, was an early Indian scout and fur trapper who had married Lisette of the Walla Walla tribe about 1830, and had a farm two miles east of St. Paul. Marguerite Liard went to school in St. Paul and later was attending school in Fort Vancouver when General Grant was there after the Civil War. During the summer vacations she helped flail the wheat on her father's farm.

In 1871, Adolph Jette, 46, and Marguerite Liard, 19, were married in the church in St. Paul.

In 1873, Mr. and Mrs. Jette moved into the Newell house near the Pelland-Larocque Store and Warehouse. This was to be their home for many years. In 1879, they purchased the store and warehouse on credit. The business, one of the largest in Marion County, consisted of a grocery, general merchandise and farm implement store, and two warehouses. Customers came from St. Paul, Butteville, Woodburn, St. Louis and Gervais. The Jettes were able to pay for the store and warehouse from the profits made during the first year.

After several years Mrs. Jette decided that the young people of the surrounding community needed a dance hall, so the Jettes converted the 150 feet by 40 feet two-story wool warehouse to a hall. Mrs. Jette had strict rules that there would be no drinking in the dance hall area. The cost per couple was $1.25 and included a ham dinner with apple pie. As many as 250 couples would come each Saturday evening, staying until two o'clock in the morning. The Barney, Giesy and Allen brothers played for the dances. Andy Labonte of St. Paul played the violin, and it was said that "one note from his violin could break your heart". People came by carriage, by haywagon, on horseback, on foot, and even by steamboat from Portland.

The Jette store was a stagecoach stop and Mr. Jette had the Champoeg Post Office for 24 years. Several years after Mr. Jette purchased the store and warehouse, a Mr. Statts, who had operated a saloon nearby, decided to retire. Mr. Jette bought the saloon and modernized it so that it gained a reputation as one of the finest saloons in Marion County.

The Jettes lost 2,000 bushels of wheat in the flood of 1890, when the water rose so high that steamboats docked at their store. At the time of the panic of 1893, Mr. Jette sold his complete stock of goods on credit because customers had no cash. When the panic passed every single customer paid in full.

Mr. and Mrs. Jette had nine children, as follows: Charles W. A., who married Elizabeth Thededaux, a native of Minnesota and, after she died, Mrs. Maybell Stratton

Fickering of Drummon,Wisconsin; Albert J., who remained
single; Frank A., who married Mildred Reynolds of Mc-
Minnville and, after she died, Delia (Smith) Jaynes of
Dallas, Oregon; Arthur F., who married Bertha Engle of
Woodburn; Lillian, who married Charles Burgoyne of
Castle Rock, Washington; Alvina, who married Albert
Smithson of Portland; Azilda, who married Paul Miller of
Salem; Edna, who married Mr. Lowrey; and Elsie, who
married John Lang of Ohio.

Mr. Jette died in 1917 at the age of 91. Mrs. Jette died in
1931 when 80 years of age.

Mr. and Mrs. Jette both spoke English, French and
Chinook. They believed strongly in education. All four
of their sons attended Mt. Angel College, and the five
girls went to Mt. Angel Normal School. Mr. Jette always
appeared in a white shirt, and his diction is said to have
been flawless. Mrs. Jette acted as a midwife and comforted
the sick as far away as Hillsboro. The Jettes were very
successful in business, were friendly to everyone, and were
greatly respected because of the many contributions they
made to the community in which they lived.

Seventeen-year-old Frank "Babe" Jette
sitting on an empty beer keg in 1897

Frank Jette Collection

JOHN JOHNSTON AND
MARY (KENNEDY) JOHNSTON

The John Johnston Family

Charles Johnston Collection

John Johnston, the son of Thomas and Hannah Johnston, was born in County Tyrone, Ireland, in 1828. His family came to America in 1835 and settled in St. Louis, Missouri, where his father was in the commission business. John was educated in private schools. When he was fifteen, he and his brother started to work in a flour mill in Beardstown, Illinois.

In 1850, John, 22, and two friends, Horace Hill and Dan Riddle, decided to come to Oregon. They bought four yoke of oxen and in April 1850 they started their westward journey from Independence, Missouri. They arrived in Marion County in August. After arriving, John Johnston obtained employment at James McKay's Mission Mills. After about a year, he went to Yreka, California. Pack horses were used for the trip. After prospecting in the mines near there for a short while, he returned to Oregon and ran a mill on the Santiam River. Later, in 1852, he and William W. West purchased 490 acres about three miles southeast of St. Paul, just east of Champoeg Creek, from Matthew McCormick. There was a little log cabin on the land, and he and Mr. West lived there and did their own housekeeping for the next four years.

Mary Kennedy, daughter of John Kennedy and Catherine (McCabe) Kennedy, crossed the plains in 1847 with the John and Barney Kennedy families when she was five years old. Her mother died before reaching Oregon. She was raised for a time by her aunt and uncle, Barney and Arah Kennedy.

John Johnston, 28, and Mary Kennedy, 14, were married in 1856. After the wedding, the couple settled on Mr. Johnston's farm. Eventually they purchased Mr. West's interest, and owned the entire original 490 acres. By 1890, they had expanded their farm to 535 acres. Over the years it was necessary to clear the land, and eventually they had one of the most productive farms in the area. They raised wheat, oats, hops, cattle and hogs, and also some racing horses.

John and Mary (Kennedy) Johnston had eleven children, as follows: Ellen, who married K. Manning of Portland; Mary Anne, who married Charles Henkle of Portland; Thomas, who married Nettie Wyland of Mollala; Robert Amety; Sara Agnes; William Patrick, who married Nancy Bailey of Salem; John, who remained single; Joseph Alexander, who remained single; Charles Perry, who married Margaret Johnson of Portland; Eliza Margaret, who married Fred Kinns of Woodburn; and Cecelia Anna, who married Mr. O'Neill of Gervais.

John Johnston died on November 2, 1912, at the age of 84. Mary, his wife, lived until April 3, 1925. She was 83 at the time of her death.

The John Johnstons were one of the most prominent families in the St. Paul area. They loved social activities, and participated enthusiastically in the cultural and social life of the area. Mr. Johnston was always interested in improving the community. He was clerk of the local school board for twenty years, and for many years was Roads Supervisor for the area. Mary (Kennedy) Johnston exemplified the prominent part that women played in the development of a high quality civilization in the state of Oregon.

DANIEL KAVANAUGH AND
CATHERINE (DOYLE) KAVANAUGH

Mr. and Mrs. Daniel Kavanaugh and Family

Clarence Kavanaugh Collection

Daniel Kavanaugh was born in County Dublin, Ireland, on December 22, 1831. He became an orphan as a young boy and spent his early teens near historic Culert Hill in County Wexford. In 1849, when he was 18, he came to the United States and settled with an uncle in Janesville, Wisconsin. He later obtained a job driving supply trains for the U.S. Government. For about ten years he hauled supplies with oxen across the plains to Fort Laramie and Fort Bridger. On one of these trips the caravan became snowed in in Utah and the party was rescued by Brigham Young.

Catherine Doyle was born in Boris, County Carlow, Ireland, in 1837. She grew up on a farm in a large family of modest means. As a young girl she met Daniel Kavanaugh, who was six years older than she was. After he went to the United States they corresponded with one another, and when she was 19 she decided she was going to the United States.

As she did not have enough money to pay for the trip, one day, without telling her parents, she took one of her father's cows and sold it for fifteen pounds. She then purchased passage to the United States, but had to wait at the docks because the next sailing was several days away. When the family discovered that she and the cow were missing they started looking for her and found her near the docks. Her father told her that if she wanted to go that badly he would forgive her for the theft of the cow. She then returned home for a farewell celebration before returning to the docks and sailing for America. After arriving she settled in Janesville, Wisconsin.

On February 12, 1860, Daniel Kavanaugh, 29, and Catherine Doyle, 23, were married in Beloit, Wisconsin. Almost immediately after their wedding they left for Oregon via the Isthmus of Panama. They arrived in Portland in October 1860 and proceeded up the Willamette River to French Prairie. There they purchased a small farm about eight miles southeast of St. Paul and a half mile south of the St. Louis Catholic Church, where the first Mass had been celebrated on December 25, 1847.

Over the years the Kavanaughs continued to farm and purchased additional tracts of land. Eventually they had considerable acreage, but some of their land was of poor quality and difficult to farm. As a result they went through some very hard times, and occasionally had difficulty raising money for seed for the next year's crop.

Mr. and Mrs. Kavanaugh were strong disciplinarians. On several occasions Mrs. Kavanaugh threw her son Andrew's belongings out the window because he wanted to marry a girl of whom she did not approve. Once, when John, another son, was in his teens and ploughing on one of the farms at noontime, after eating his lunch, he strolled off into the woods with his rifle to hunt for a few minutes. When he returned there were no horses and no plow where he had left them. He looked down the field and saw that his father had hitched the horses to the plow and was ploughing. When Mr. Kavanaugh arrived back where John was, he gave the reins to him and said, "I guess I'll have to hire a man to plough this field", and walked away.

For many years, Andrew, the eldest son, who obtained a law degree, and his brother Edward assisted their father with the operation of the farms. John obtained his bachelor's degree with the first graduating class at Mt. Angel College and later graduated from law school at the University of Oregon. He was a prominent Portland attorney for many years, City Attorney of Portland, and Judge of the Circuit Court. He received the rarely given "DeSmet Medal" from Gonzaga University for his legal work in connection with the successful fight against the Ku Klux Klan-sponsored Oregon School Bill before the U.S. Supreme Court in 1922. He was a partner in the law firm of Kavanaugh and Bowerman and was prominent in Republican Party circles in Oregon for many years. Henry received his degree in medicine and settled in Pendleton, where he became one of the leading doctors in eastern Oregon. Edward's son Clarence attended the University of Washington. He was an early day radio announcer and later became an actor and director of note. He directed and acted in the Cleveland Playhouse for more than twenty years and later directed and acted in such plays as "Annie Get Your Gun" and "Anastasia" in Daytona Beach, Houston, Memphis and Nashville, and acted on Broadway in New York in "Advise and Consent". His sister Elizabeth became Sister Philomena Kavanaugh of the Servants of the Holy Heart of Mary in Kankakee, Illinois. Mary Kavanaugh taught school in Oregon for almost fifty years.

Mr. and Mrs. Daniel Kavanaugh had eight children, as follows: Andrew, who remained single; Anna, who married William McKay of St. Paul; Sarah, who married Elmer Savage of Salem; Martha, who married A. L. Clark, who became principal of Astoria High School; John, who married Eleanor Dunn of Portland; Henry, who married Katherine Murray of Portland; Edward, who married Nettie Newton of St. Louis; and Mary, who remained single. They also raised an orphan girl and treated her as if she were one of their own.

The Kavanaugh family was intelligent, highly respected and very serious about their religion. They believed in giving their children the best education possible. The characteristics which seemed to distinguish them most were an exceptionally good sense of humor and the constant desire of each of them to express his or her opinion in the friendly conversations that inevitably seemed to occur when one of them was part of a group of people.

BARNEY KENNEDY AND ARAH (UNDERWOOD) KENNEDY AND JOHN KENNEDY AND CATHERINE (McCABE) KENNEDY

William Kennedy, Mrs. Barney Kennedy and Sarah Kennedy

Cecil Smith Collection

Barney and John Kennedy were born in Blown Rock, County Donegal, Ireland. Barney was born in 1811 and John in 1813. As young men they crossed the Atlantic to Canada, where they lived for several years. They eventually moved to Joliet, Illinois.

Arah Underwood was born in Orange County, Indiana, on February 10, 1819. She later moved to Joliet with her family. In February 1839, Arah Underwood, 20, and Barney Kennedy, 27, were married in Joliet. After the wedding the young couple moved to Louisa County, Iowa.

John Kennedy eventually moved from Joliet to Missouri. While in Missouri he married Catherine McCabe. On December 23, 1842, while the couple were living in Memphis, Missouri, a daughter Mary was born. At some time between then and September 1847, Mrs. John Kennedy died.

In the spring of 1847, Mr. and Mrs. Barney Kennedy and their two-year old son John, and John Kennedy and his five-year old daughter Mary, and possibly Mrs. John Kennedy, left Louisa County, Iowa, for Oregon. Each of the brothers had a covered wagon with three yoke of oxen. They crossed the Missouri River at St. Joseph, Missouri. After enduring many hardships and much suffering on the long journey, the Kennedys arrived in St. Paul in September 1847.

Mr. and Mrs. Barney Kennedy purchased a 640 acre land claim from a Mr. Doughrain. The family moved into a small round log cabin on their land, which eventually became the Barney Kennedy Donation Land Claim. John Kennedy took up a 320 acre land claim just south of his brother's claim. Both claims, which became their farms, were located about three miles east of the St. Paul Mission on the east side of Champoeg Creek. It is probable that John Kennedy and his daughter, Mary, lived with the Barney Kennedys for the first several years after they arrived in Oregon. After a time the Kennedys built a hewed log house on Barney Kennedy's property.

In the spring of 1848, John Kennedy went to the California gold fields with a party which included Hugh Cosgrove and Mr. and Mrs. James McKay, who were his closest neighbors. After a successful adventure the party returned to St. Paul in December of 1848.

In the spring of 1849, Barney Kennedy went to the California gold fields with a party that included the Hugh Cosgroves. He crossed the mountains with pack mules.

After a very successful season in the gold fields he returned to St. Paul in late fall of the same year.

Barney and John Kennedy were also very successful in their farming operations. Barney's farm was eventually expanded to 1,200 acres. After Barney Kennedy died in 1865, his wife and five children continued to run the general farming and stock raising operation.

On September 9, 1867, Mr. and Mrs. Barney Kennedy's son John, 22, who was known as John Kennedy, Jr., married Julia Scollard, 18, in the St. Louis Catholic Church. Julia had crossed the plains a year earlier with her parents, the Maurice Scollards, who had a farm about five miles southeast of St. Paul. After the wedding the young couple purchased a farm south of the Barney Kennedy farm. Their farming operation, which included a large hop field, was very successful. John Kennedy, Jr. had considerable mechanical ability, and he was one of the first farmers in the area to own a threshing machine. The John Kennedy, Jr.'s had four children, as follows: Anna, who married Bernard "Ben" Smith of St. Paul; Margaret, who married Fred Miller of Woodburn; Joseph, who married Frances Murphy of Silverton; and Thomas, who married Stella Walsh of Silverton.

After Barney Kennedy died, one of his children, Thomas, died while a young man. From that time Mrs. Arah Kennedy, her son William and daughters Mary and Sarah continued to expand their large farming operation, which included hop yards, until 1904 when they retired in Woodburn. William, Mary and Sarah remained single. Sarah, the youngest, was given much credit for the successful operation of the large farm.

In 1849, John Kennedy, Barney's brother, whose first wife had died, married Mary Poujade, the daughter of Dr. Poujade of St. Louis, Oregon. She died seven months later and he found himself a widower again. In 1858, his only child, Mary, married John Johnston, a native of Ireland who had come to St. Paul in 1850. After working at the Mission Mill for James McKay, and later successfully prospecting for gold in California, Mr. Johnston purchased a 500 acre farm just south of Mary's father's claim. John

Kennedy married for the third time when he was about 45. His wife's name was Isabel, and she was a native of Ireland.

Barney Kennedy died on December 28, 1865, when he was 54 years of age. Mrs. Arah (Underwood) Kennedy outlived her husband by almost 30 years, dying on May 18, 1904. John Kennedy, Sr. died January 24, 1884, at 64 years of age.

The Barney and John Kennedys and their children were very active in the social, cultural and religious affairs in the St. Paul community. Because they lived on the east side of Champoeg Creek they attended church in St. Louis most of the time. Arah Kennedy's parents were Quakers but she never joined any church. Her children were raised in the Catholic religion. After Woodburn was established about 1870, the Kennedys made many significant contributions to that community. Barney and John Kennedy were known for their wit, their rich Irish nature, their adventurous spirit and their capacity for hard work. Arah (Underwood) Kennedy, because of her sociability and charitable nature and her broad-minded perspective on life, was recognized as one of the outstanding individuals in the St. Paul area.

St. Paul Baseball Team—about 1910

JOHN D. KENNEDY AND
BRIDGET (NAGLE) KENNEDY

Mr. and Mrs. John E. Kennedy

Lucille Kennedy Sturgeon Collection

John D. Kennedy was born in 1820, in County Kilkenny, Ireland. He came to the United States as a young man and settled in Dubuque, Iowa.

Bridget Nagle was born in New York of Irish immigrant parents in 1831, and subsequently moved to Dubuque, Iowa.

John D. Kennedy, 27, and Bridget Nagle, 16, were married in Dubuque on April 3, 1847. After the wedding the young couple moved to the Bluegrass region of Kentucky, where two daughters, Margaret and Alice, were born. They later returned to Iowa where a third daughter, Mary, was born in 1853. In 1854, the family crossed the plains and settled in Harrisburg in Lane County, Oregon. They operated a farm there and later purchased another farm near Coberg in Lane County. In the late 1860's, the John D. Kennedy family moved to St. Paul and purchased a 173 acre farm about one mile northwest of the town. They lived there for the next twenty years. The Kennedys were interested in race horses and owned several of the fastest horses in Marion County. Their first child born in Oregon, Eliza, was the fourth native-born Oregonian to become a member of the Sisters of the Holy Names when she entered from

St. Paul in 1872. She took the name of Sister Mary Raphael. The two boys in the family, John E. and Edward, operated farms in the St. Paul area for many years.

The John D. Kennedys had ten children, as follows: Margaret, who married Mr. Darnielle of Boyd, Oregon; Alice, who married Mr. Cox of Athens, Oregon; Mary, who married John Coleman of St. Paul; Eliza, who became Sr. Mary Raphael; Annie, who married Mr. Johnson of Tacoma, Washington; Amanda, who remained single; Caroline, who married Daniel Murphy of St. Paul; Elizabeth, who married Mr. Hansen of Portland; John E., who married Lucy Connor of St. Paul; and James, who remained single.

John D. Kennedy died in Portland, Oregon, on August 4, 1897, when 77 years of age. Bridget (Nagle) Kennedy died in 1918, at the age of 87.

The John D. Kennedys were a very prominent St. Paul family. Mr. Kennedy was known as the Honorable John D. Kennedy and their home was one of the finest in the community. About 1890, Mr. and Mrs. Kennedy retired and moved to Portland. Their children were all active participants in the social, religious and cultural activities of the area. After John E. Kennedy and Lucy Connor were married, their nephews, such as Caroline Kennedy's son, Arthur Murphy, who lived in Portland, would spend the summers working on the John E. Kennedy farm.

PETER KIRK AND
MARGARET (LYON) KIRK

Mr. and Mrs. Peter Kirk and two of their children

St. Paul Mission Historical Society

Peter Kirk, the son of Thomas Kirk and Marcella (Lyon) Kirk, was born in Clogherhead, County Louth, Ireland, in 1830. His father had two brothers: George Harley Kirk, who was a poet and a member of the British Parliament; and James Kirk, who came to the United States and became a New York City Police Commissioner. Peter Kirk came to America at the age of 20 in 1850.

Margaret Lyon was born in Killarney, County Kerry, Ireland, in 1832. She came to the United States with her mother, Mrs. Helen Lyon, when she was 16 in 1848.

In 1854, Peter Kirk, 24, and Margaret Lyon, 22, were married in Boston, Massachusetts. They lived there for three years, during which time two children, Elizabeth and Thomas, were born. The family moved to Minnesota in 1857 and purchased a 160 acre farm near St. Mary's, a small town near Waseka. It was difficult to make a living there as the soil was poor and the nearest market was about 30 miles away. At times Mr. Kirk made the sixty-mile round trip and received only 40 cents per bushel for his wheat.

Because of the small income being received from the farming operation, Mr. Kirk decided to leave his family in Minnesota and join a 200-man wagon train which was going to Montana to prospect in the mining area there. After arriving in Montana he decided to establish a shoe making shop. He brought in supplies for his shoemaking business by pack horse, and business grew so rapidly that in three years he had accumulated a small fortune. He then returned to Minnesota, where his wife and young family had operated the farm during his absence, and the family decided to come west.

In 1870, Mr. and Mrs. Kirk and their children, and Mrs. Kirk's mother, came to Oregon via the new transcontinental railroad, which was less than a year old. After their arrival in St. Paul they purchased a 345 acre farm about a half mile north of the town. A year after they arrived, Mr. Kirk purchased the Jesuit Mission property for his friend and neighbor in Minnesota, Matthew Connor.

The Kirks suffered a great loss in 1873 when Mrs. Kirk died. The eldest daughter, Elizabeth, suddenly found that she was very busy caring for her eight younger brothers and sisters. That year Mr. Kirk's father, Thomas Kirk, came from Ireland to St. Paul. He lived with the Kirks until his death a year later. In 1875, Peter Kirk married Margaret Gargan.

In 1878, Mr. Kirk built a large warehouse on his farm. The warehouse stood near the eventual site of the narrow gauge railroad's St. Paul station, and one of the Kirk sons, R. E. "Emmett", was later appointed St. Paul agent for the railroad. In about 1880, Mr. Kirk and Emmett built a general merchandise store just northeast of the St. Paul church. In 1879, two other Kirk sons, Thomas and John, purchased 250 acres about a half mile east of St. Paul, just east of

Mission Creek. This was eventually expanded to 400 acres and later divided between the two brothers. They built a large home on the property, which still stands today. They raised wheat, oats, corn, clover, hops, horses, cattle, sheep and hogs; and the farming operation was very successful. One of John Kirk's sons, Urban J., was later to establish Twin Oaks Poultry Farm on part of this property. He became president of the Oregon Branch of the National Poultry Association and was one of the first to sell baby chicks and hatching eggs from chickens that had been trapnested, that is, identified by the number of eggs the hen had laid each year. The hatching eggs were sold throughout the western part of the United States and many of the baby chicks were delivered by air. R. E. "Emmett" Kirk's daughter, Hazel, married Alva Blackerby, who later became United States Forest Service Supervisor for the Nez Perce National Forest.

Peter Kirk had five brothers and sisters. His sister Jane married Patrick Gately and one of their daughters, Georgie, became Sr. Loretta of the Sisters of Providence. She held the post of Director of the Educational Department for that order. One of his brothers, John, settled in Spokane, Washington, and there was much visiting back and forth between the St. Paul and Spokane Kirks.

After Peter Kirk's second wife, Margaret (Gargan) Kirk, died, he married Matilda Dixon. Peter Kirk died in 1897, when 66 years of age.

Peter Kirk and Mrs. Margaret (Lyon) Kirk had eleven children: Elizabeth, who married James Murphy of St. Paul; Thomas, who remained single; John, who married Cecelia McKay; R. E. "Emmett", who married Agatha McDonald of St. Paul; Richard, who married Jennie Smith of Portland; Peter, Jr., who married Mary Merten of St. Paul; Mary Agnes, who remained single; James, who died when 19 years of age; Margaret, who died when 6 years old; and Mary J. and an infant, who died in Minnesota.

Peter and Margaret (Gargan) Kirk had one daughter, Margaret, who remained single. Peter and Matilda (Dixon) Kirk had one son, Joseph, who married Julia Keeney of

Portland, Olive Livers of Portland, and after her death
Juanita "May" Bellanger of Taft.

The Peter Kirks became one of the leading families in
St. Paul. They were distinguished by their resourcefulness,
hard work and a good sense of humor. Their eldest daughter
Elizabeth lived to be 99 years of age. Up until the time she
was 85, several times each week she would walk through the
various 20 acre fields on her farm with her cane and man's
style flat hat, and pump water for the livestock from wells
located on each of the fields. John Kirk's eldest daughter
Geraldine was a teacher for 50 years, and has been a life-
long supporter of the various Catholic charities in Oregon.

Interior of R.E. Kirk Store

Hazel Blackerby Collection

LOUIS LABONTE II AND
JOSETTE (LAFRAMBOISE) LABONTE

Louis Labonte II

Oregon Historical Society

Louis Labonte II was born near Astoria in 1818. He was the son of Louis Labonte I, who was born in La Prairie, Canada, and either an unknown Indian woman or Kilakotah, the eldest daughter of Chief Coboway of the Clatsop Indians. (When the marriage of Louis Labonte I to Kilakotah was legitimized by Father Blanchet at St. Paul in 1839, part of the record shows "Legitimizing Louis Labonte II aged 20 years by a former marriage". Other records indicate that Kilakotah was his mother.)

Louis Labonte I arrived in Astoria with the Wilson Price Hunt Party of the Astor Expedition. The expedition left Montreal in July 1810, followed roughly the route of Lewis and Clark, and after many harrowing experiences arrived at Astoria on February 15, 1812. Louis stayed in the Astoria area until about 1818, when his son Louis Labonte II was born there. After Louis Labonte arrived in 1812, he worked for the Astor group's Pacific Fur Company, the Northwest Fur Company and the Hudson's Bay Company. In 1828, when his contract with the Hudson's Bay Company expired, he requested that he be allowed to stay in the Willamette

Valley. In accordance with company policy this request was denied. He left his ten-year old son with his wife, Kilakotah—who also had a six-year old daughter, Victoire McMillan, by a previous marriage—and left for Montreal. Eighteen months later, having completed the 8,000 mile round trip to Montreal, he rejoined his wife and the two children, after having obtained his formal discharge. He then asked Dr. McLoughlin if he could start a farm.

Dr. McLoughlin, who admired his determination to live in the Willamette Valley, gave him the few things which were necessary to start a farm. Louis then brought Kilakotah, whose Indian name meant "Little Song Bird", and the two children to French Prairie. Accounts indicate that they moved in with the Joseph Gervais family about 8 miles south of St. Paul near Chemaway. Kilakotah's younger sister, Yaimust, was the wife of Joseph Gervais. In about 1836, after having lived in various locations, the Labontes took up a land claim in Yamhill County directly west of St. Paul on the west side of the Willamette. Mr. Labonte described his farm as embracing all the area that a man could ride around in one day on a good Cayuse horse. In 1841, when making an inspection for the U.S. Government, Lt. Wilkes reported that Louis Labonte's farm was the best he had seen in the Willamette Valley.

Louis Labonte II married Caroline Montour of French Prairie in 1843. All of their children probably died when young. He went to the gold fields in 1848 or 1849. His wife died in 1851. In 1852, he married a daughter of Jean Baptiste Gervais of French Prairie. She died in 1854. He then served with the Oregon Volunteers in the Indian War of 1855-56.

Josette Laframboise was the daughter of Michel Laframboise and Emilie Picard. Michel Laframboise had arrived in Astoria in 1811 on the ill-fated Astor Party steamship TONQUIN. He later worked as an interpreter and explorer for the Northwest Fur Company and the Hudson's Bay Company, and he was sent on many dangerous missions. He may have been the most colorful of all the French Canadians in the Willamette Valley. Josette's mother, Emilie Picard, was the daughter of Andre Picard of Quebec,

Canada, who had come west with the Northwest Fur Company. He was later a postmaster for the Hudson's Bay Company and was one of the earliest settlers in the Willamette Valley.

On April 1, 1856, Louis Labonte II, 37, and Josette Laframboise, 18, were married in the St. Paul Catholic Church. The couple settled in the St. Paul area sometime between 1860 and 1880.

Louis Labonte II and Josette (Laframboise) Labonte had seven children, as follows: Louis III, who married Josephine Belleque of St. Paul; Francois, who died when young; Jean Baptiste, who remained single and died when 21; Andre, who remained single; Antoine, who died when 17; Nazairre, who remained single; and Josephite, who married David Gregoire of St. Louis, Oregon. Mr. Gregoire was a son of Victoire McMillan and a grandson of Kilakotah Labonte.

Josette (Laframboise) Labonte died when 40 years of age in 1879, and Louis Labonte II died in 1911, when 93.

The Labontes were a very prominent St. Paul family. Before Louis Labonte I died at age 80 in 1860, he had on several occasions been in financial difficulty and had found it necessary to mortgage his half of the farm. Kilakotah would never mortgage her half. Finally, she gave her portion to the husband of her daughter Victoire (McMillan) Gregoire with the understanding that Victoire would take care of her in her old age. She was probably about 75 years old when she died in 1873. Julienne, the daughter of Louis Labonte I and Kilakotah, was a very beautiful girl and married Narcisse Vivet, Jr. in 1858. Louis Labonte II became a prominent member of the Oregon Pioneer Association and proudly wore his ribbon with "1818", his year of birth, on it. One of the Louis Labonte II's sons, Andre Labonte, was a talented vocalist and sang at many St. Paul social affairs. Louis Labonte II and Josette descended from parents who had carved homes out of the wilderness at a time when even log houses were a rarity. They were strong and daring and contributed greatly to the civilization which developed in the Oregon Country, the Oregon Territory and the state of Oregon.

FRANCOIS LAMBERT AND CLEMENTINE (MONGRAIN) LAMBERT

Mr. and Mrs. Francois Lambert

Beverly Lambert Bush Collection

Francois Lambert was the son of Augustin Lambert and Catherine (Pichet) Lambert.

Augustin Lambert came to Oregon with the Hudson's Bay Company about 1840, when he was 27 years of age. He was the son of Severin Lambert and Claire Lebrun, who were married in Montreal on the 24th of July, 1809, at St. Michel of Yamaska.

Augustin's paternal grandparents were Pierre Noel Lambert and Therese Aral; his maternal grandparents were Bonaventure Lebrun and Marguerite Couturier. All apparently came to Montreal from France.

Augustin married Catherine Pichet of Montreal. They then went to Red River, Canada. Mrs. Lambert remained there to await the birth of their first child, while Mr. Lambert went on to Oregon.

After arriving Augustin took up a land claim about eight miles southeast of St. Paul. This was probably in the year 1840. On this claim he built a log cabin. He cleared and worked the land for five years and then returned to Canada to bring his wife and son to their new home. With his wife now at his side he continued farming, and eventually branched out into logging. These logging operations were to become quite extensive and were carried on by three generations of the family.

Most of the logs from their "logging camps" were sold to large Portland furniture manufacturing companies. These logs were towed down the river by the Lamberts with their own tugs, making it a complete operation from the cutting to the delivery.

Francois was born and grew up on his father's farm, where he helped with the logging business.

Clementine Mongrain was a daughter of David Mongrain and Catherine (Lafantaisie) Mongrain, who had a farm about two and one-half miles southeast of St. Paul by the early 1840's. Catherine Lafantaisie was the daughter of Jacques Lafantaisie, who came to Astoria on the ill-fated steamship TONQUIN in 1811, and Suzanne of the Okanogan Indian Nation.

Francois Lambert and Clementine Mongrain were married on January 1, 1877. Francois' and Clementine's fathers both had voted at Champoeg on May 2, 1843. They represented families that had a genuine interest in the future of the Oregon Country. After the marriage, the Lamberts continued extensive logging, sometimes with Pierre Kitson, who had married Angelique Dupre. Angelique was the daughter of Catherine Lafantaisie by a previous marriage.

Francois had nine brothers and sisters; however, only four grew to adulthood. Augustin II married Marguerite Sanders; Marie married Francois Bernier II; Antoine, who did not marry, died at the age of 25; and Alfred married Matilda Crete.

The Francois Lamberts had nine children, as follows: Ramey "Remi", who married Dorothea Brooke; Amina, who married Charles Fellers; Caroline, who married George Faber; Mary Celina, who married Emil Digman; Edward, who married Mary Flannagan; August, who married Anna Sanko; Bertha, who married Frank Siefert and later Harry Endicott; David, who died when about two years of age; and Frank, who died at the age of 20.

In addition to the logging, the Lamberts also had a hotel where a "pot au feu" was always on the stove for anybody who stopped by. This hotel, which gave the Lamberts a great opportunity to become acquainted with a large part of the population, still stands today about a block east of the St. Paul Post Office.

In 1913, one of Frank Lambert's brothers, Alfred, patented a peavey, which is used to roll logs. Since that time it has been one of the basic logging implements used throughout the United States. He also had a saloon and was one of the better baseball players in the St. Paul area.

Clementine Mongrain Lambert died in 1924 at the age of 67, and Frank Lambert died in 1932 when 83 years of age.

The Lamberts were a busy family, but always had time for fun and laughter. They were noted for their sense of humor, and had many friends throughout the area. Francois "Frank" Lambert was affectionately known by the St. Paul citizens as "Pogie" Lambert.

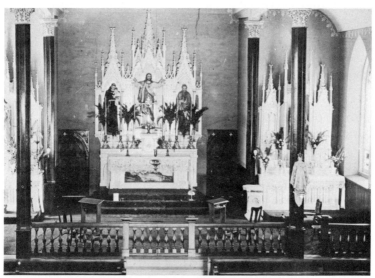

Altar installed in the St. Paul Catholic Church after the renovation of the church in 1890

St. Paul Mission Historical Society

DIEU DONNE MANEGRE AND
EMELIE (PICHET) MANEGRE

Mr. and Mrs. Dieu Donne Manegre

Louise Mucken Manegre Collection

Dieu Donne Manegre, the eldest son of Pierre Manegre and Judith (Chevrette) Manegre, was born in Winnipeg, Canada, in 1831. When he was 17 years old he and four friends left Canada and went to the California gold fields via Cape Horn. After mining for about five years, four of the party and Adolph Jette, a friend from Canada they had met in California, decided to go to French Prairie in Oregon.

One night on the Siskiyou Trail, which was very hard to follow because there was snow on the ground at the time, a young Indian girl sneaked up to their campfire and warned them that the Indians were coming at dawn to kill them and take their gold dust, which they were carrying in their buckskin belts. They hurriedly packed and left their campsite. The Indian girl asked them to take her with them as she was afraid she would be killed for warning them. They did take her with them, and she was very helpful as she knew how to cover their tracks, follow the trail and trap wild game. Finally they arrived at Louis Pichet's Log Inn about three miles southeast of St. Paul. Mr. Pichet said that the Indian girl could stay with his family, because he knew that no Indian tribe would take her. Dieu Donne Manegre, after staying at the Log Inn for a while, bought some land from Louis Pichet and built a small log house near a spring of pure water.

Emelie Pichet was born in St. Paul in 1845. Her father, Louis Pichet, was born in St. Ours, Montreal, and came to Oregon about 1820. After fur trapping for a while he became a courier for the Hudson's Bay Company. He settled on a farm three miles southeast of St. Paul about 1835. Emelie's mother, Marguerite Bercier, was born about 1817 and was the daughter of Antoine Bercier, who came west with the Northwest Fur Company, and Emelie (Fenlay) Bercier. Emelie Fenlay's father, Francois Fenlay, had married Giget of the Cree Indian Nation about 1790 and changed her name to Josephite. He was probably a fur trapper in the northern Rocky Mountains as early as 1775. Emelie Fenlay was probably born in western Canada about 1795. Francois Fenlay eventually worked for the Northwest Fur Company, and later as a courier and trapper for the Hudson's Bay Company.

Emelie Pichet's father, Louis Pichet, built a large two-story log house on his farm; and it became an inn, or stopping place, for people newly arrived in or passing through St. Paul or St. Louis, Oregon.

On January 6, 1861, Dieu Donne Manegre, 30, and Emelie Pichet, 16, were married in St. Paul.

The couple lived on Mr. Manegre's farm about two and one-half miles southeast of St. Paul. They eventually expanded their farm to 265 acres. They were successful farmers and became quite wealthy over a period of years.

Mr. Manegre retired in 1890 and turned the farm over to his children.

The Dieu Donne Manegres had eleven children, as follows: Louis, who remained single; Sevare, who married Alice Vandale of St. Paul; Narcisse, who remained single; Peter, who remained single; Amelia, who married George Aplin of St. Paul; Mary, who married Matose Fortier from Canada; Margaret, who married Joseph Puru from Canada; John, who married Irene Johnson, a native of Michigan; Rosa, who married Christian Grohs from Germany; Amanda, who married Jesse Allen Wallace of Cowlitz Valley, Washington, and after he died, Wilburn Gunnoe; and Michelle, who died when an infant.

Dieu Donne Manegre died at age 72 in 1903. Emelie (Pichet) Manegre died in 1919 when 74 years of age.

The Dieu Donne Manegres were loved and respected by all who knew them. They were friendly, cooperative, enthusiastic and had a lively sense of humor. One of their sons, John, had a large machine shop in St. Paul. Their youngest daughter, Amanda Lorraine, was an artist and painter of considerable note. When Dieu Donne Manegre died in St. Paul his funeral was one of the largest in the community up to that time.

The Mongrain Brothers

Beverly Lambert Bush Collection

MATTHEW McCORMICK AND JOHANNA (CLANCY) McCORMICK

Mr. and Mrs. Matthew McCormick

Margaret Reichenbach Collection

Matthew McCormick was born in County Meath, Ireland, on December 12, 1820. When he was seven years old he came to the United States with his parents, the Patrick McCormicks. The family settled in Genesee County, New York, where they purchased a farm. When Matthew was 15 he became an apprentice with a cabinet maker in Rochester, New York. At the age of 21 he enlisted in the United States Infantry and served in the Mexican War. He was wounded above the left knee at the Battle of Monterey while charging to take a battery. After being hospitalized for several months he was discharged at New Orleans. He then went to St. Louis, Missouri, where he served on the police force for one year.

Johanna Clancy was born in Ireland in 1822. She came to the United States with her family. The Clancys settled in St. Louis, Missouri.

In 1846, Matthew McCormick, 26, and Johanna Clancy, 24, were married in St. Louis.

After the marriage Matthew McCormick worked as a blacksmith and wagon manufacturer. By the spring of 1849, the McCormicks had three children and they decided to go to the California gold fields. They obtained five yoke of oxen, a covered wagon and provisions. During the course of their westward journey all three of their children died. Arriving in California in October 1849, they prospected and mined near the Feather River for the remainder of the year, then in January of 1850 embarked on a schooner for Oregon. The journey took three weeks, as they encountered severe storms en route. They initially stayed in Milwaukie and then came to St. Paul, where they resided for about a year. They then purchased the Larocque donation land claim about five miles southeast of St. Paul, paying $1,000 for the property. The land was almost entirely timbered and included a log house. Eventually, after the long process of clearing the land, they had a large farm. They operated the farm for many years and produced abundant crops of grain and hops and fine herds of cattle.

Mr. and Mrs. McCormick had seven children, as follows: three young children who died during the journey across the plains to California; John, who married Katherine McKay of St. Paul; Charles, who married Mary Van Wessenhove of Champoeg; and Mary and Josephine, who died within eight days of one another from diphtheria when they were twelve and fourteen years of age in the spring of 1865.

Mrs. McCormick died at age 65 in 1887, and Mr. McCormick died in 1907 when 87 years of age.

Mr. and Mrs. Matthew McCormick were enterprising, energetic and friendly. They loved social affairs. Their integrity was unquestioned and they contributed greatly to the community in which they lived. They were devout members of the St. Louis, Oregon Catholic Church. One of the sons attended St. Lawrence College in Montreal, Canada, and both were talented musicians. Charles had an orchestra for many years and John was the church organist at St. Louis for forty years.

John Manegre and Fred Raymond on their bicycles—about 1900

St. Paul Mission Historical Society Collection

MILES McDONALD AND
MARIA (GALLOWAY) McDONALD

Mrs. Miles McDonald   The McDonald Daughters

Hazel Blackerby Collection

Miles McDonald was born in Armagh, County Armagh, Ireland, in 1810, the son of Owen McDonald and Mary (McKeon) McDonald. He came to the United States and eventually came to Oregon in 1846 via steamship around Cape Horn. He helped build the Catholic brick church in St. Paul and later worked for Archbishop Blanchet at the mission mills. In late 1847, he took up a land claim near Little Muddy Creek in Yamhill County. He moved to the claim in early 1848 and started building a log house, but returned to St. Paul in late spring and supervised the operation of the Mission Mills during the six months when James McKay was in the California gold fields. He then returned to Yamhill County, completed his log house and started his farm.

Maria Galloway, born in Juneau, Wisconsin, in 1834, was the daughter of Charles Galloway, a native of Hamshire County, Virginia and Mary (Heeney) Galloway, a native of Ireland who came to America with her parents when she was 7 years old. The Galloways were married in 1830, and in 1832, Mr. Galloway enlisted for the Blackhawk Indian War and served in that war. Maria Galloway's paternal grandfather, who fought in the Revolutionary War, was present at Yorktown and saw Cornwallis surrender to George Washington.

In 1852, the Charles Galloway family decided to come west and crossed the great plains by ox-drawn covered wagon. Mr. and Mrs. Galloway and their eight children left in the spring and arrived in Oregon after a seven months' journey. This was the year of the cholera epidemic. One of their children died on the plains, and a brother-in-law died near the Platte River. After arriving in Oregon the Galloways took up a land claim near Amity in Yamhill County. They built a house, started clearing land; and Maria, then 18, lived there with her parents and brothers and sisters for the next three years.

On October 15, 1855, Miles McDonald, 45, and Maria Galloway, 21, were married in the Catholic Church at St. Paul.

The couple first lived on Mr. McDonald's farm in Yamhill County, but eventually purchased a farm just east of the St. Paul Catholic Church. This farm became their home for many years. After Miles McDonald's death in 1876, Mrs. McDonald and the children continued to operate the farm. One of the sons, Peter, was the St. Paul Postmaster for 34 years. During the depression of the 1930's, he put in a stock of goods and operated a combined post office-general merchandise store, which he operated until he retired at age 70 in 1944. A daughter, Agatha, married R. E. "Emmett" Kirk of St. Paul, who became St. Paul agent for the narrow gauge railroad in 1880 and operated a general merchandise store in St. Paul for almost fifty years. Another daughter, Veronica, married Nels Lind and their daughter, Lessie, married Charles Shea of Portland, who became president of Six Companies, Inc. This company built Hoover Dam and eventually became Kaiser Industries and built many ships during World War II. Mrs. McDonald's brother, William Galloway, was the Democratic Party nominee for Governor of the State of Oregon in 1894 after many years of service in the Oregon Legislature. Another brother, Thomas Galloway, served in the Idaho Territorial Legislature and was one of the founders of Weiser, Idaho. A third brother was killed in the Civil War.

Mr. and Mrs. Miles McDonald had eight children, as follows: Bridget "Betty", who married Mr. Pembrooke of Bloomington, Illinois; Ellen, who married William Shaw of Belfast, Maine; Agatha, who married Emmett Kirk of St. Paul; Monica, who married Frank Durant of Woodburn; Veronica, who married Nels Lind of Sweden; Theckla, who married Harry Talbot, a hop buyer from Salem; Sebastian "Sy", who married Mary Schneider of St. Paul; and Ignatius "Peter", who married Theresa Merten of St. Paul.

Miles McDonald died in 1876 at age 66. After his death Maria McDonald's mother, Mrs. Charles Galloway, came to St. Paul and stayed with her daughter until she died in 1884. Maria McDonald died in 1907, when 73 years of age.

The McDonalds were greatly interested in community affairs. They consistently participated in the social, cultural and religious activity in the community. They believed in education, participated in sports, loved their family and had a good sense of humor. Miles McDonald, in addition to helping build the brick church, served as godfather for many of the early American immigrants who were baptized in the St. Paul Catholic Church during the late 1840's and early 1850's. Maria (Galloway) McDonald was one of the most loved and respected citizens of the community.

Matthew McCormick and his very distinctive beard—about 1870

Margaret Reichenbach Collection

JAMES McKAY AND
CECELIA (LAWSON) McKAY

Mr. and Mrs. James McKay

Margaret Reichenbach Collection

James McKay, the youngest of three children born to John Neil and Catherine (McKusker) McKay, was born near Belfast, Northern Ireland, on April 15, 1818. When he was one year old the family moved to Glasgow, Scotland, where he grew up and was educated. He learned the carpenter and miller trades, subsequently obtained a position as ship's carpenter in Dundee, Scotland, and later became a foreman in a manufacturing plant there.

Cecelia Lawson, the eighth of ten children born to William and Mary (Hill) Lawson, was born on November 8, 1822, at the family home near Broughty Ferry, Scotland, which is near Dundee. Her father was a prominent manufacturer of Dundee and a representative of one of the old families of Scotland.

On June 14, 1840, when James McKay was 22 and working as a foreman in one of William Lawson's enterprises, he and Cecelia Lawson, then 18, eloped and were married in Dundee. The elopement occurred because James McKay was a Catholic and Cecelia Lawson was Presbyterian, a religious difference which provoked opposition from both families. Coming to the United States, the couple settled in Albany, New York, where Mr. McKay obtained work as a ship's carpenter.

The couple became interested in the possibility of pioneering in the Middle West. They moved to Joliet, Illinois, where Mr. McKay soon found employment on the canal being built there. While living in Illinois the McKays became the parents of two sons. The couple began to read stories written by a newspaperman who was in the Oregon Country, but who had previously been with the *Joliet Courier*. As a result they and twelve other families from Joliet decided to cross the plains to Oregon in 1847. Included in the group were the James McKays, the Hugh Cosgroves, John Hunt and Lot Whitcomb.

After obtaining covered wagons, ox teams and necessary provisions, the group left Joliet in the early spring of 1847. When the party arrived at The Dalles the members had varying opinions about the best route to the Willamette Valley. The Cosgroves decided to rent several small boats and go down the Columbia River. All the others in the party, except the McKays, decided to cross the mountains in their wagons. The McKays could not afford to rent a boat so built a raft and floated down the Columbia River to present day Portland. They arrived without their two young sons, who had died from the measles near The Dalles. After arriving in Portland in the fall of 1847, the couple went up the Willamette Valley to St. Paul. James McKay obtained employment at the Mission Mills. James Coleman and Miles McDonald also worked at the mills that fall and winter.

On January 28, 1848, James McKay purchased the mill property known as the Old Mission Mill from Archbishop Blanchet for $8,000. The archbishop had purchased the mill property from the Hudson's Bay Company in 1845. James McKay had very little money, but his promise to pay from earnings was accepted. He also purchased a section of land, a timbered tract adjacent to the mills, so that he would have logs for the sawmill which he would operate in addition to the one-bur flour mill.

Shortly thereafter word was received that gold had been discovered in California. Mr. McKay decided to try his luck in the gold fields and Miles McDonald agreed to supervise the operation of the mills in his absence.

On May 20, 1848, Mrs. McKay was baptized in the St. Paul church with Archbishop Blanchet as her godfather and Mrs. Hugh Cosgrove as her godmother. Shortly thereafter, Mr. and Mrs. McKay left for the newly discovered gold fields with a party that included Hugh Cosgrove and John Kennedy. They were among the first outsiders to arrive at the gold fields. The McKays set up a combination tavern and store near Sutter's Fort at Sacramento, which was about 25 miles from where gold had been discovered in the American River near Coloma. Mrs. McKay wrote letters for illiterate miners and was paid in gold dust or gold nuggets. After netting in excess of $10,000 in about six months, the McKays returned to the mill property in St. Paul in December 1848. The successful venture to the gold fields enabled them to pay Archbishop Blanchet the $8,000 for the mill property and also to invest money in the expansion of the operation of the mills.

In the twenty-two month period from March 1, 1847 to December 1848, the McKays had made a 2,500 mile covered wagon trip from Joliet, Illinois to St. Paul, Oregon, lost their two children, purchased a flour mill, a sawmill and a tract of land, made a 1,000 mile round trip by covered wagon from St. Paul to Sacramento, California, and made sufficient money from the gold adventure to completely pay for the mill property and have money left over.

James McKay operated the Mission Mills, which were located about three miles east of St. Paul on Champoeg Creek, for about forty years. The flour mill originally had one bur and could produce about 100 barrels of flour a day. In the spring and summer of 1861, it was renovated and expanded to a two-bur mill capable of producing twice that much. After the Champoeg Mills were ruined by the flood of 1861, the Mission Mills became one of the two largest flour mills in Marion County. Flour was shipped as far away as the gold fields in California, Jacksonville, eastern Oregon, and Idaho, by mule train or steamboat.

In 1859, James McKay purchased 160 acres of the Lebrun land claim about two miles southeast of St. Paul, and later purchased parts of the James Cosgrove and Adolphus Chamberlain land claims about three miles northeast of St. Paul. At one time he had about 1,400 acres under cultivation in the St. Paul area. In 1865, he purchased the southwest corner of Third and Stark Street in Portland for $2,750 from William S. Ladd and Charles O. Tilton. In 1888, Mr. McKay retired and moved into the Old Revere House which was located on his Third and Stark Street property. In 1892, he constructed one of Portland's most modern office buildings, the McKay Building, at that location. He also owned the southwest corner of Fourth and Yamhill Street and had property in The Dalles.

The McKays' eldest son, William R. McKay, was born in Oregon on December 30, 1849, and baptized in the St. Paul Church the same day. During the summer when he was ten years old, when drivers were hauling flour to Salem, he would do the same with his gentle team of horses. When he and brother John were in their teens they delivered flour by mule team to eastern and southern Oregon. Each brother later had about 640 acres under cultivation in the St. Paul area—two of the most productive farms in the community. Prior to his death in 1950 at the age of 100, William McKay was the oldest living individual born of American immigrants in Oregon. His daughter Estelle, who became Sr. M. Estelle of the Sisters of the Holy Names, was one of the leaders in the Holy Name Province in Oregon.

Eight children were born to Mr. and Mrs. McKay after they arrived in Oregon: William R., who married Anna Kavanaugh of St. Louis, Oregon; Mary, who remained single; Katherine, who married John McCormick of West Woodburn; John Neil, who married Caroline Bochsler of Mt. Angel; Cecelia, who married John Kirk of St. Paul; twins, who died at birth; and James, who died in early childhood.

Cecelia (Lawson) McKay died on June 13, 1870, at the age of 47 years, from complications resulting from "gold dust" fever which she had contracted in Sacramento in 1848. The eldest daughter, Mary, then acted as housekeeper and hostess for James McKay until his death at the age of 80 in 1898.

The McKays were morally strong, adventurous, courageous, honest and farsighted. They were one of the earliest pioneer families of the Oregon Territory and contributed greatly to the social, cultural and religious affairs of the community of St. Paul. Their Mission Mills added to the development of commerce and industry in the state of Oregon.

Sixteen-year-old William McKay shortly before leaving for Santa Clara University in 1866

Joseph McKay Collection

STEPHEN MERTEN AND
THERESIA (GOODING) MERTEN

Mr. and Mrs. Stephen Merten

Eileen Kaufmann Collection

Stephen Merten was born in 1842, near the German border in Merten, Alsace-Lorraine. He and his brother, Matthew, came to the United States in order to avoid the military drafts. They settled in Minnesota.

Theresia Gooding was born in Indiana. Her parents had come from Alsace-Lorraine and had settled on a farm near Mt. Vernon, Indiana. After the death of her father and mother, Theresia moved to Minnesota to live with her uncle, John Gooding.

In 1877, Stephen Merten, 25, and Theresia Gooding, 19, were married in St. Anne's, Minnesota.

The couple and Mr. Merten's brother, Matthew, then came west and settled near Austin, Nevada, where they took up government land and operated a cattle ranch. Stephen Merten also obtained rights to gold mining property, so that venture helped finance his farming operation. The combined operations were rather successful. In 1889, after three daughters had been born to the Mertens, they decided to look for a farming area where better educational opportunities were available. The only school near them in Nevada was the Paiute Indian School, and as it was five miles away from their home, the children attended school infrequently.

The Mertens sold their ranch, which was later to become part of the Indian reservation, and most of their cattle at a good profit and set out for the Willamette Valley by wagon and on horseback. The two eldest girls rode horseback and herded eleven cows. After arriving in the Willamette Valley they camped near Salem for several days while Mr. Merten looked over the countryside. The Stephen Mertens selected acreage one-half mile south of St. Paul and established their farm there. Matthew Merten settled in Portland.

The three daughters of Stephen Merten enrolled at St. Paul Academy. They were much older than their classmates. They studied music, art and needlework in addition to academic subjects.

The Mertens operated their farm successfully for many years, and their family became an integral part of the cultural, social and religious life of the community. Mr. Merten and his sons hauled building materials for many weeks when St. Paul Academy was rebuilt after a fire in 1910.

The Stephen Mertens had eight children, as follows: Elizabeth, who married Eugene Davidson of St. Paul; Mary, who married Peter Kirk of St. Paul, and after he died, Charles Mullen of St. Paul; Theresa, who married Peter McDonald of St. Paul; Clara, who married John "Jack" Davidson of St. Paul; George, who married Anne Kuensting of Broadacres; Stephen, who married Angela Hughes of St. Paul; Irene, who married Dr. Raymond Jones of McMinnville; and Maurice, who married Mary McKay of St. Paul.

Mr. Merten died at 76 years of age in February 1928, and Mrs. Merten died May 31, 1941, at age 84.

In her later years, Mrs. Merten was known to all in the community as "Grandma Merten". She lived an active life to the last, taking part in all civic activities and enjoying her home and flower gardens. Mr. and Mrs. Merten always tried to hold to the values and principles which guided the Oregon pioneers. The large sculpture in the St. Paul

Church, copied from Michaelangelo's Pieta, which was donated by Stephen and Theresia (Gooding) Merten, is an example of their contributions to the St. Paul community.

Amanda "Mandy" Raymond about 1900

Dolores Bustamonte Collection

Hugh Burns, who carried the first mail across the great plains in 1846

Joseph McKay Collection

PATRICK MULLEN AND
MARY (FLYNN) MULLEN

Mr. and Mrs. Patrick Mullen

Charles Mullen Collection

Patrick Mullen was born in Ireland, on November 1, 1839. He was the son of Thomas Mullen, a native of Kildare, County Kildare, and Mary (McNebbin) Mullen, who was born in Dublin. Mrs. Mullen had previously been married to a Mr. Keaton; and a son by that marriage, Robert Keaton, had come to the United States as a young man. He arrived in Oregon on October 30, 1852, and took up a land claim of 160 acres about one mile north of St. Paul.

In 1851, Mr. and Mrs. Mullen and Patrick left Ireland for the United States. They first lived in New Orleans for about a year and then moved to St. Louis, Missouri, where for five years Mr. Mullen was a cook in various hotels. While they were in Missouri, Robert Keaton wrote letters to his mother suggesting that the family come to Oregon. They moved to Illinois, where Mr. Mullen died of pneumonia in 1859. After Mr. Mullen's death Mrs. Mullen and Patrick boarded a steamer at New Orleans and left for Oregon. They came via Havana, the Isthmus of Panama, and San Francisco and arrived in St. Paul on Christmas Eve of 1859. They lived with Robert Keaton in his small log house and helped him operate his farm.

In 1870, Robert Keaton decided to try his luck in the Idaho gold mines. He left with his team, mining equipment and necessary provisions but was never seen again. His family surmised that he was possibly captured and killed by marauding Indians. Patrick Mullen continued to operate his half-brother's farm and also cleared additional land.

Mary Ann Flynn was born in Albany, New York, on October 22, 1855. She was the daughter of Bernard and Catherine (Bennett) Flynn, both natives of Ireland. The Flynns came to Oregon in 1857 and purchased land about four miles northeast of St. Paul. During the trip across the plains some Indians stole Mary Ann, who was just able to walk at the time, and Mr. Flynn had to plead with the Indians and give them a sack of grain and some smoked meat in order to get her back. She grew up on Mr. Flynn's farm.

On November 10, 1880, Patrick Mullen, 41, and Mary Ann Flynn, 25, were married in the St. Paul Catholic Church.

The couple lived on Patrick Mullen's farm in a large frame house which had been built about 1875. The house, which has had some additions, still stands today. As time went on the Mullens purchased additional land. Eventually their farm contained 240 acres and extended to the bank of the Willamette River. At one time they had thirty Chinese workers from Portland helping clear their land. While clearing the land the Mullens found such things as arrowheads, chips from rocks used as tools by the Indians, shining rocks and ashes from bonfires. Their farm was one of the finest in the St. Paul area.

In addition to farming, Patrick Mullen purchased horses and wagons and established a transportation business. He hauled grain and produce from all parts of the Willamette Valley to Portland. Later he raised horses and sold them to coal hauling businesses in Portland and seine fishermen in Astoria.

The Patrick Mullens had nine children: Philip A., who married Jennie Hughes of St. Paul; Charles, who married Mary Merten of St. Paul; Mary, who married Edgar Eubanks of Portland; Katherine, who married Henry Tillman of Portland; Joseph, who married Marjorie Anderson of Newberg; Thomas, who remained single; Irene, who married Harland Hartzell of Portland; and Cecelia, who married Joseph Volk of Portland.

Patrick Mullen died at the age of 82 in March 1920. Mary Ann (Flynn) Mullen died three days later, at age 65.

The Mullens were very successful in their various enterprises. Their eldest son, Charles "Charley" Mullen, was in attendance when St. Paul Academy was converted to a co-educational elementary school in 1892. He was one of the leaders in the drive to obtain a public high school for St. Paul, and when St. Paul High School was established in 1923 he was named chairman of the school board. He retained the position for many years. He presently lives in the house his father built about 1875. For many years Patrick Mullen took up the collections in the St. Paul Church. He was proud of his assistance to the priests, the Holy Names Sisters and the orphans in the St. Paul orphanage. Mrs. Mullen was a loving mother and a strong support for her husband. One of the stained glass windows in the St. Paul Catholic Church shows the names of two of its early supporters, Patrick and Mary Ann (Flynn) Mullen.

Joseph Gooding and his new car in front of a St. Paul saloon—about 1910

Jean Abner Collection

MATTHEW O'CONNELL MURPHY AND MARY ELLEN (COSTELLO) MURPHY

Mr. and Mrs. Matthew Murphy

Matthew Murphy Collection   *Harvey McKay Collection*

Matthew O. Murphy, the eldest of six children born to Daniel Murphy of Banadluck Parish, Killmuckridge, County Wexford, Ireland and Catherine (Dillon) Murphy of Clonmel, County Tipperary, Ireland, was born on June 19, 1830, in Galena, Illinois.

Matthew's grandfather, Andrew Murphy, who owned a large estate in County Wexford, had taken a prominent part in the Wexford Rebellion of 1798. This involvement was probably the reason the family left Ireland and came to the United States in 1799. At that time Matthew's father, Daniel, was about 10 years old. The family settled in Galena and worked in the lead mines in that vicinity. Eventually Daniel surveyed public lands in the area which is now Peoria and Peru, Illinois, and later became a member of a surveying expedition which surveyed the Santa Fe Trail in the Indian territory.

Matthew Murphy's mother, Catherine (Dillon) Murphy, was the granddaughter of Thomas Hanly of Armfield,

County Tipperary, Ireland, who was an officer under Wellington in Spain during the Napoleonic War. When Catherine's mother, Margaret (Hanly) Dillon, became a widow with seven children, Catherine's uncle, John Hanly, brought his sister and her children to St. Louis, Missouri, where Catherine grew up.

In 1828, Daniel Murphy, about 40, and Catherine Dillon, 19, were married in St. Louis. Matthew O'Connell Murphy was born two years later in Galena. When Matthew was fourteen his father's business failure caused severe financial handicaps for the family, and for three years young Matthew worked virtually from dawn till darkness for various employers and received little more than bare subsistence. In September 1848, news of the California gold discovery reached St. Louis and every young man, Matthew included, who could raise the price of an outfit, was determined to go to the gold fields the next spring.

Early the next spring Matthew, three of his cousins and two friends each put up $325 for the adventure. They purchased a wagon, six mules and provisions and gave free passage to an expert mule skinner. They made the trip from St. Joseph, Missouri to Placerville, California in 120 days. After being fairly successful Matthew returned to St. Louis in early 1851. Shortly thereafter Matthew, his parents, and two brothers, Daniel and Peter, set out for Oregon via the Isthmus of Panama. As they passed through Portland in the summer of 1851, Mr. and Mrs. Daniel Murphy purchased two lots at what is now the corner of Fourth and Taylor Streets, but which then was little more than a cleared patch in the timber.

Matthew took up a 320 acre land claim about a mile north of St. Paul and his father took up an adjacent 640 acre land claim. Matthew built a small house near the river on his claim.

Mary Ellen Costello, the fourth of six children born to John Costello of County Meath, Ireland and Ellen (Burns) Costello of Tyrellspass, County Westmeath, Ireland, was born on May 15, 1836, in the Old Council House in Fort Wayne, Indiana. Mary Ellen's uncle, Hugh Burns, came to Oregon in 1842. Her father died in 1847, when she was eleven years old. She attended the public school and the Convent of Notre Dame boarding school in Fort Wayne. In 1849, her mother married John Gearin, a neighbor whose wife had died and left him with a family of young children. Encouraged by glowing letters received from Mary Ellen's uncle, Hugh Burns, the family decided to go to Oregon.

In May 1851, John Gearin, his wife Ellen, Ellen Gearin, Mary Ellen Costello and her brothers, John and Michael, and 18-month old Hugh Gearin, left Fort Wayne. They arrived in St. Paul in the fall of that year. After arriving they built a small log house on their claim. Mary Ellen stayed with her uncle, Hugh Burns, and attended the Sisters of Notre Dame School in Oregon City.

Matthew Murphy and Mary Ellen Costello were married in the St. Paul Catholic Church on February 4, 1856.

After the wedding the couple settled in their home near the river. Shortly after their third child, Daniel, was born, on April 16, 1860, they were forced to evacuate their home by a devastating Willamette River flood. Mary Ellen was lifted out of a second-story window with her two-day old baby, Daniel, in her arms. The flood swept away all their possessions, including their farm animals. Shortly afterward Matthew obtained a position as assistant head surveyor of a group conducting surveys in the Washington Territory. While a survey of Whitby Island was nearing completion, the chief surveyor and some of his men were murdered by an Indian chief. Matthew then took charge and escaped with the remainder of the party to the Yessler Blockhouse near Seattle. He later conducted land surveys for the U.S. Government in Oregon and Washington for many years, while at the same time operating his farm at St. Paul.

The Matthew Murphys believed strongly in education. Their sons, James and Daniel, graduated from St. Mary's College in San Francisco, and their daughters all attended St. Mary's Academy in Portland. Their eldest son, James, was an early day teacher in the St. Paul area. He later had a butcher shop in Sprague, Washington, and eventually took over the operation of the farm at St. Paul. Two of James Murphy's daughters became members of the Sisters of the Holy Names. Elizabeth became Sr. Elena and Agnes became Sr. Agnesia. Sr. Agnesia received her Masters Degree from Gonzaga University and was recognized as one of the most outstanding and most popular high school teachers in the Holy Names Sisters' schools in the Pacific Northwest. The Matthew Murphys' eldest daughter, Katherine, became Sr. Alodia. She was a convent superior for many years and was one of the early leaders in the Oregon Province of the Sisters of the Holy Names. Daniel, the second son, was Chairman of the Democratic Party in Oregon in 1892, became U.S. Attorney for Oregon in 1893, and was a prominent attorney in Portland for many years. His son, Arthur Murphy, worked his way through Stanford University and was president of the student body there. He was a captain in the U.S. Army in France during World War I, was one of the founders of the American Legion, was Vice-President in charge of Western Operations for the Union Pacific Railroad, and President of the Seattle Chamber of Commerce. Susan Murphy married Philip Kelly, who was a co-founder of the Kelly-Clark Co., and pioneered in vacuum-packing salmon in Alaska. Joseph Murphy's son, Matthew, became a colonel in the U.S. Army, and was the Staff Intelligence Officer for Headquarters, Fourth Army in San Francisco during World War II.

Matthew and Mary Ellen Murphy had fourteen children, as follows: James, who married Elizabeth Kirk of St. Paul; Katherine, who became Sister Alodia of the Holy Names Sisters; Daniel, who married Caroline Kennedy of St. Paul; Mary Ellen, who died when 5 years old; William, who married Emma Coleman of St. Paul; Matthew, who married Mary Ann Culross of Sprague, Washington; Albert, who died when a young man; Mary Agnes, who died when 2 years old; Lucy, who married Dr. William Turner of Santa Barbara, California; Susan, who married Philip Kelly of Seattle; John, who married Olive Looney of Tacoma; Joseph, who married Ella Birdsong of Oregon City; Octavia, who remained single; and Eugene, who died when a baby.

Matthew's brother, Daniel Raphael Murphy, married Susan Harrison of Eugene and the family settled in Salem. His other brother, Peter Kenrick Murphy, married Martha

Johan O'Connor of St. Paul, and the family eventually settled in Spokane, Washington.

Matthew Murphy died on May 27, 1906, when 75 years of age. Mary Ellen Murphy died when 76 on December 2, 1912.

The Matthew Murphys were a prominent St. Paul family. Like the majority of the residents they grew most of their own food on their farm, and their main cash crops were wheat and oats. Mrs. Murphy purchased cloth and made clothing which the family wore. Their library contained the works of Milton, Shakespeare, Scott and Thackeray. They were greatly interested in literature and Matthew read aloud to the family until the day he died. The Murphy family participated enthusiastically in the social, cultural and religious affairs of the community.

Students at the St. Paul Public Grade School—about 1890

St. Paul Mission Historical Society

CHARLES O. PELLAND AND
MARY E. (COLEMAN) PELLAND

The Charles O. Pelland Family

Charles Pelland Collection

Charles O. Pelland was born in Montreal, Canada, on September 17, 1840. He came to Oregon in 1860 and settled in Oregon City, where he was engaged in the milling business for eight years in partnership with Mr. George Larocque, who had previously been an Indian scout and fur trapper. In 1868, Pelland and Larocque established a mercantile business about four miles northeast of St. Paul above where Champoeg had been before the 1861 flood. This business rapidly developed into one of the largest mercantile businesses in Marion County.

Mary E. Coleman of St. Paul was born in Yamhill County in 1851, the daughter of Mr. and Mrs. James Coleman. Her parents crossed the plains in 1847, lived in St. Paul for a short while, then took up a claim in Yamhill County. Later, they sold the Yamhill property and returned to St. Paul.

On New Year's Day of 1873, Charles O. Pelland, 32, and Mary E. Coleman, 21, were married in St. Paul.

After the wedding the couple lived near Mr. Pelland's store. In 1879, after Pelland and Larocque sold their mercantile store to Adolph Jette, the Pellands moved to Newport, Oregon, where they operated a mercantile store for about a year. In 1880, they purchased a farm in Yamhill County where they stayed until 1882, when they returned to St. Paul. They established a mercantile store about two blocks from the church on the southeast corner of the main intersection. They operated the store until 1889, when they sold it to Herman Waltz and Joseph Gooding. The Pellands then purchased a 400 acre farm about 3 miles south of St. Paul, where they produced abundant crops and lived for the remainder of their lives.

The Charles O. Pellands had eight children, as follows: Charles A., who married Mary Gratton of Portland; Florence G., who married Alfred Daly of Seattle; George, who died during childhood; Fred J.; Marie, who married Dr. Fred Newsome of Athena, Oregon; Philip O., who married Myra Woods of Lostine, Oregon; Helen, who married Fred J. Hill of Seattle; and Gerald, who married Romana Johanson of Seattle.

Charles O. Pelland died at age 64 on May 31, 1904, and Mary Pelland died in 1930 when 89 years of age.

The Pellands were good conversationalists who loved social affairs and horse racing and who had great success in their business ventures. Their children's weddings were all gala affairs which were enjoyed by the St. Paul community. Mrs. Pelland had the reputation of being able to make the best bread pudding in the Pacific Northwest.

CHARLES F. RAY AND
AMELIA (EYRE) RAY

Mr. and Mrs. Charles F. Ray

Florence Lull Collection

Charles F. Ray was born in Saratoga County, New York, on August 8, 1829. He arrived in St. Paul in 1850. During 1850, he operated a ferry at Deguire's Landing. The ferry, which had been established in 1826 by the Hudson's Bay Company, was perhaps the first ferry across the Willamette River. That same year, 1850, Mr. Ray started operating the Oregon City-Salem mail route. He carried mail and passengers on his Conestoga wagon and passed through Champoeg and St. Paul on each trip.

Amelia Eyre was born in Sheffield, England, about 1835. She was the youngest daughter of Miles and Eliza Eyre, who had a cutlery business in Sheffield. In about 1842, the

Eyres came to St. Louis, Missouri, and, with a partner, established a cutlery business there. In 1843, they left the partner in charge of the business and crossed the plains. They had a good outfit and plenty of money, but tragedy struck when Mr. Eyre was drowned at the second crossing of the Snake River. He had several thousand dollars in his money belt. The wagon train camped for three days but were unable to find his body or the money belt. As a result, Mrs. Eyre was left with four children and $13. To further complicate matters, the eldest daughter, Mary, was riding with friends near the head of the train and the wagon she was with was part of a group which chose to follow a sign that said "California". The rest of the party, including Mrs. Eyre and three other children, took the route to Oregon. By the time Mary received the sad news it was too late for her to join the rest of the family, so she stayed with her friends and went to California. News of the tragedy travelled fast, and when Dr. McLoughlin heard of Mrs. Eyre's plight he sent a party of Indians with a boat to meet her at The Dalles. The Indians brought Mrs. Eyre and the three children to Fort Vancouver, where they spent the winter. She washed clothes for the soldiers, sewed and did other chores to earn board and room for herself and her young family. Those at the fort did everything possible to assure that the Eyres were comfortable.

In 1844, the Eyres went to the Waldo Hills area, where they built a cabin and lived until 1848. They heard from Mary about 1845. At one time some Indians were attracted to Amelia, the youngest daughter, because of her red hair which hung in long curls. When Mrs. Eyre wouldn't sell her the Indians tried to steal her, and the family had to constantly watch her so she wouldn't be stolen. On another occasion the other daughter, Eliza, took a position as a companion to a family of white children in Lapwai and escaped the Whitman Massacre by returning to Waldo Hills just two weeks before that unhappy event. In 1849, the Eyres went to California, and together with Mary and her husband returned to the east. One day before they reached New Orleans Mary's husband died. They continued on to Boston, where they stayed for about a year. In 1850, Mrs.

Eyre and the three younger children, Thomas, Eliza and
Amelia, again crossed the plains to Oregon.

In 1852, Charles F. Ray, 23, and Amelia Eyre, about 18,
were married.

Mr. Ray eventually expanded the mail route and stagecoach service until it ran from Portland to Corvallis. He also
built and operated the first livery stable in Salem. In the fall
of 1869, the Rays rented the Deguire Donation Land Claim,
which G. C. Davidson had purchased in 1857 but had been
unable to continue operating because of the great financial
losses suffered in the 1861 flood.

The Rays moved into the large house which the Davidsons had built. It contained two large fireplaces, one in the
living room and the other in the dining room. The house
was very sturdily built, with the boards in the wall being
about two inches thick and probably handsawed. In 1873,
the Rays bought the farm, which included the ferry and
landing, and from that time forward the landing became
known as Ray's Ferry and Landing. The spot became the
river terminal for the narrow gauge railroad. Several large
shops were built there, as well as shops for the railroad
workers. The high water of 1890 washed out the railroad
tracks in the area and the operation of the railroad and ferry
was discontinued shortly thereafter. However, the Rays
continued to operate their large farm on the bank of the
Willamette River for many years.

Charles F. and Amelia (Eyre) Ray had fourteen children.
They were as follows: Mary Frances, who married Mr.
Apperson of Portland and later John A. Holmes; Henrietta
"Ettie", who married James Coyle, who had a blacksmith
shop in St. Paul; Amelia "Millie", who married Wallace
Mauzier of Portland and later Allan Tucker of Seattle;
Alice, who married Captain Sherman Short of Portland;
Ada, who married Edward Wilkinson, a Portland engineer;
Hazel, who married a Portland jeweler, Harley Morton;
William, who remained single; Walter, who married
Lillian Shively of Oregon City and later Fay Lamson; Inez,
who married Clay Harrison of Portland and later James
Smith of San Francisco; John, who was a druggist in Port-
land; Charles, who married Daisey Sandstone; Maude, who

married Mr. Burnett and later Mr. Nessler; Guy, who married Hazel Kinnon; and Frank, who died when 7 months of age.

Amelia (Eyre) Ray died at age 75 on March 20, 1909. Charles F. Ray died on June 28, 1919, at the age of 89. The Charles F. Rays were a leading family in the St. Paul area. With their early stage coaches and Ray's Ferry and Landing they spurred the development of transportation in the Willamette Valley. They and their large family contributed greatly to the social and cultural life of the community.

St. Paul Centennial—1939

St. Paul Mission Historical Society

AUGUSTIN RAYMOND AND
MARIE (SERVANT) RAYMOND

Mrs. Augustin Raymond

Dolores Bustamonte Collection

Augustin Raymond was born on April 19, 1811, the son of Toussaint Raymond and Marie (Biscornet) Raymond, who had a farm in St. Cypriene, Montreal, Canada. He came to Oregon about 1835 and took up a land claim about a mile and one-half south-southeast of St. Paul. He built a log cabin on the land, which was heavily timbered, and started clearing the land which was to become his farm.

Marie Servant was the daughter of Jacques Servant and Josephite of the Okanogan Indian tribe. She was born about 1830. Her father, Jacques Servant, was born in 1795 in Montreal, Canada, and came to Oregon between 1810 and 1815, perhaps with the Astor Party. By the late 1830's, he had a large farm about one mile south-southeast of St. Paul. On November 6, 1843, Augustin Raymond and Marie Servant were married in the St. Paul Catholic Church. F. X. Matthiew was one of the witnesses at the wedding. After the wedding the couple settled on Mr. Raymond's farm, which was just south of Mrs. Raymond's father's farm. On June 2, 1854, Mrs. Raymond's father, Jacques Servant, died. He left a large portion of his extensive holdings to Mrs. Raymond. The Raymonds continued to clear additional land and expand their farming operation. By 1870 the Raymonds had ten children. After Augustin's death on October 12, 1873, the 1100 acre farm was divided equally into ten 110 acre farms—one for each of the ten children.

One of the Augustin Raymonds' daughters, Emelie Caroline, married Julien Provost, who came to St. Paul in the 1840's and was a teacher at St. Joseph's College. Mr. Provost became the first mayor of St. Paul in 1905, drew up the city charter and mapped out the streets. One of Augustin Raymond, Jr.'s sons, Henry Raymond, was one of the better baseball players in the area in the early 1900's.

The Augustin Raymonds had ten children, as follows: Joseph; Marcelle, who married Odille Raymond of St. Paul; Emelie Caroline, who married Julien Provost of St. Paul; Augustin, Jr., who married Josephine Mongrain of St. Paul; Francois, who married Angelica Dupre of St. Paul; Alexander; Rosalie, who married Isaac Crete of St. Louis and later Mr. Bergevin of St. Paul; Salome, who married Eusebe Forcier of St. Paul; Alfred; and Madeline, who married Mr. Payne.

Augustin Raymond died on October 12, 1873, at the age of 62.

The Augustin Raymonds had one of the largest and finest early day farms in the St. Paul area. They made a special contribution to St. Paul in the form of music. Augustin Raymond donated the first organ that was in the St. Paul Church, and his daughter Emelie Caroline was the first church organist. The family played an important part in the social, religious, civic and cultural affairs of early day St. Paul.

FRANCIS S. SMITH AND
ELLEN (NOLAN) SMITH

The Francis Smith Family

Mark Smith Collection

Francis S. Smith was born in County Cavan, Ireland, in 1826. He was the son of Francis S. Smith and Catherine (Morgan) Smith, who had a farm near Lurgon Parish in County Cavan. After his mother died his father eventually decided to marry another woman whom Francis S. Smith, Jr. and his brothers and sisters did not like. As a result the five children, Francis S., Charles, Bernard, Elizabeth, and Rose, decided to come to the United States.

They arrived in Philadelphia on July 29, 1850. Francis S., who was then 24 years old, eventually settled in Dubuque, Iowa. His two sisters, Elizabeth and Rose, probably accompanied him there. One brother, Charles, went to the southern part of the United States. The other brother, Bernard, who was 17, had applied, while in Ireland, to the Holy Cross Congregation to be a brother. Almost immediately after arriving in the United States, he went to South Bend,

Indiana, where he was accepted as a brother in the Congregation of the Holy Cross at Notre Dame University. He was later to be named as manager of the farm at Notre Dame and held that position for many years. Elizabeth and Rose both took their habits as Catholic nuns the same day at St. Catherine's Convent at Benicia, California, in 1864—Elizabeth as a Dominican sister and Rose as a Sister of Mercy.

Ellen Nolan was born in County Kilkenny, Ireland, on November 19, 1842. She came to the United States with her parents when she was five years old. The Nolan family settled on a farm near Dubuque, where Ellen was raised.

About 1862, Francis S. Smith, 36, and Ellen Nolan, 20, were married in Dubuque.

The couple was living in Dubuque in 1863 when Mr. Smith received his notice to report for duty for the Civil War. He paid an individual $25 to take his place, which was legal at that time. He subsequently received another draft notice and this time paid an individual $100 to take his place. At this time the Smiths, who had a young son, Charles, decided to go west.

They sailed down the Mississippi River, took a steamship to the Isthmus of Panama, which they crossed on a new narrow gauge railroad, and proceeded to San Francisco by steamship. After their arrival in San Francisco they took up a homestead claim. Part of the claim later became part of Golden Gate Park. They stayed there for about a year and while there a second son, Bernard, was born. Shortly thereafter Mr. Smith decided to drive a herd of horses to Corvallis, Oregon. Mrs. Smith and the two young boys accompanied him in a wagon. After living in Corvallis for about a year they decided to move to St. Paul. They had heard of the fertile land in the area and knew there was a Catholic church in St. Paul.

The Smiths arrived in St. Paul in 1866 and purchased a 200 acre farm about two miles northeast of St. Paul. They established a cattle ranch and eventually additional land was acquired. Later, three of the older sons, Bernard, James and Joseph, expanded the operation still further and built a slaughter house. They named the combined operation

Smith Brothers Meat Company and purchased cattle, hogs, sheep and poultry from all over French Prairie. The dressed meat was shipped by river boat from Champoeg to Portland. A younger brother, Frank, would meet the boats as the produce arrived in Portland and sell the meat to the commission houses on Front Street in Portland. Later the younger brother, Frank, established Frank L. Smith Meat Company with 28 markets in Portland, one in Seaside and one in Astoria.

Charles Smith, the eldest son, was a blacksmith by trade, lived with his mother's sister in Walla Walla, Washington, joined the Army and eventually retired as a major after service in the Spanish American War. His brother Jack also served in that war. James became the first president of the St. Paul Bank, was a W. P. A. Administrator, county judge and for many years was County Commissioner of Marion County. His son William was the first president of the St. Paul Rodeo Association. Joseph Smith's son, Leslie, was the head of the Associated Press in San Francisco in the early 1940's and his sister, Sr. Eloise Ann, was Dean of Studies at Marylhurst College. Frank Smith's son, Leo Smith, received his law degree from Georgetown University and was a member of the Oregon legislature from 1939 until 1945. He was later District Attorney of Multnomah County, received an Honorary Doctor of Law degree for legal assistance to parochial schools, and has been a prominent attorney in Portland for many years. One of Frank Smith's daughters became Sr. Elivera of the Holy Names order and another daughter became Sr. Frances A. Smith of the Sacred Heart Congregation. She graduated from Manhattanville College in New York City, received her doctorate from Fordham University, and during the course of her distinguished career taught two of President John Kennedy's sisters.

Mr. and Mrs. Francis S. Smith had eleven children, as follows: Charles, who married Mary Lynch; Bernard "Ben", who married Anne Kennedy of St. Paul; James, who married Jane Davidson of St. Paul; Joseph, who married Annie Kavanaugh of Portland; Steven, who remained single; Peter, who married Mary Ann Hughes of St. Paul; William, who married Marie Faber of Portland; Jack, who remained single; Rose Ann, who married Chauncy Hastorf of Portland; and Frank L., who married Nellie Kavanaugh of Portland.

Francis S. Smith died on May 31, 1899, at age 73, and Mrs. Ellen (Nolan) Smith died when 94 on July 3, 1936.

The Francis S. Smith family participated enthusiastically in the social, cultural and religious affairs of the community and became one of the most prominent families in the St. Paul area. Over the years the children increased their land holdings in the community; and they and their children raised cattle, grain, hops and other farm products with great success.

At the present time a fourth generation of Smiths in the community continue the family tradition—a tradition which developed and has been maintained because of a love of the land and a love of the St. Paul community.

View south on Main Street, St. Paul, Oregon, from near the center of town, in 1913. LaBelle Bakery, Clarno's Meat Market, Gooding and Waltz Store and Ernst Hardware Store are on the left. Van de Wiele's Store, State Bank of St. Paul and St. Paul Post Office-McDonald's Confectionery Store are on the right. The St. Paul Catholic Church is about one block west and facing east. The St. Paul Town Hall is two blocks east and facing north.

St. Paul Mission Historical Society Collection

PART III

INDIVIDUALS IN THEIR OWN WORDS

THE PICHET-MANEGRE FAMILY TREE

By Amanda Lorraine (Manegre) Gunnoe

"I, Amanda Lorraine Manegre, was born April 14, 1882 and next April I will be 77 years old. I am in sound mind and good memory and wish to leave a record of our family for my children, grandchildren and great-grandchildren. I will tell as much as I can remember of the true facts of our family, starting with my great-grandparents on my Mother's side and with my grandmother on my Father's side, whose name was Judish Chevrette.

The facts I am about to relate were told me when I was a child by my father and mother. I will first tell of the people on my Mother's side who were the first to settle what is now known as French Prairie in Oregon. This beautiful spot is bounded by Champoeg, Woodburn, Gervais and the Willamette River. However, it was long before the existence of these towns that my great-grandfather, Francois Fenlay, first set foot on this prairie. Though spotted at intervals with groves of tall firs, it was for the greater part clear level ground with lush grass which grew very high. It proved excellent farming ground and my great-grandfather thought this part of the country was the most beautiful place he had seen in all his travels. At this time he was working for the Hudsons' Bay Fur Company as a courier and trapper. Previously he had been with the old Northwest Fur Company. On leaving the employ of John McLoughlin, the Hudson's Bay Factor, he settled on this prairie and started farming. It was because of him and a number of other Frenchmen who, instead of returning to Canada, chose to settle here, that it became known as French Prairie. There were no white women in this country at that time so he married an Indian girl whose name was Giget. There were no churches, priests or ministers here then. Francois later gave Giget the name of Josephite. As the years went by one of their children whose name was Emelie married a Frenchman whose name was Antoine Bercier. They were my great-grandparents. These two had a daughter Marguerite and she married another Frenchman named Louis Pichet who had come from St. Ours, Montreal, Canada. They were my grandparents whom I remember very well. I was eight years old when my grandmother Marguerite Bercier Pichet died in the year 1890.

Louis Pichet, my grandfather, had taken a land grant in the French Prairie and built an extra large log house. This became a stopping place for those travelling to and from California. Many men left Oregon on the discovery of gold in California to seek their fortunes in the gold fields. Previous to this however, in 1838 on petition of these French farmers the Catholic Church sent some Catholic priests to the Oregon Country and soon a small church was built in what is now St. Paul. Immediately on arriving the priest performed marriages for these French families and thus their alliance was legalized and the children were considered truly legitimate. This was the beginning of law in this country that had been so wild.

The Indian tribes that passed through French Prairie on hunting and berrying expeditions behaved very well and the settlers treated them good and traded with them. These were honest hard working settlers who worked for the good of the country as well as for themselves.

In the year 1845, my grandmother Marguerite gave birth to a daughter who she named Emelie and she was my mother.

Now about this time on a farm not far from Quebec in Canada lived a boy of French parentage, Dieu Donne Manegre, eldest son of Pierre Manegre and Judish Chevrette. When he was about 17 years old he and four other French boys left their homes to seek gold in California. They went by sailing vessel around the Horn to San Francisco and then to the gold fields. After a few years of mining they started on the trail to Oregon. They had heard of the beautiful French Prairie from others who had left Oregon to join the Gold Rush. These men told them that the lush green grass grew waist high. It was good soil for farming and no land to clear, yet plenty of wood and timber nearby.

They were told how dangerous the Siskiyou Trail was. They had heard of travellers being killed by the Indians on this trail. So they listened to all the advice, but were undaunted. They carried what food they could and had Buckskin Belts filled with their hard-earned gold dust. Each carried a rifle and they found game very plentiful as they travelled. As they reached the Siskiyou Mountains they found the trail very hard to follow as there was a light snow on the ground. There were five of them in this group: Adolph Jette, Felix Delisle, Jim Contois, a man named Piette and my father, Dieu Donne Manegre.

One night after eating, they sat around their camp fire talking and wondering how long it would take them to make the trip to French Prairie. They had been told about the Inn that my grandfather Louis Pichet operated and they planned on stopping there first on arrival. The fire burned lower and soon they were wrapped in their blankets and asleep except for one that was the first to watch. I do not remember which man was on watch, but I know it was not my father. However, he heard a twig snap and was alert to see what it might be. He awakened one man and as they slept so that each could touch the other, they soon were all awake. Looking toward where the sound came from, they first saw an arm raise and then a form coming toward them. To their surprise it was a young Indian girl and she had come to warn them that the Indians were coming at dawn to kill and rob them of their gold. They hurriedly rolled up their belongings and as they started to leave, this Indian girl knelt on the ground in the snow and took the hand of one of the men and indicated that she wanted to go with them and show them the way. Through signs and some words she showed them she was afraid for her life because she had warned them. There was little time and they didn't know the way so they took her along. This without a doubt saved their lives as she wouldn't let them go along the trail but took them another way and she followed behind them shaking the limbs of the bushes and trees so as to cover their tracks with the snow. In her quiet way she helped all she could, even taking turns at watching during the night when they slept. She also set snares as they travelled through the country and caught grouse and rabbits in the early dawn. This helped much with their food problem and they did not have to use their guns which might have attracted the Indians to them. With this young girl's help they were able to reach their destination. At one point in the mountains they had lost the trail and were three days finding their way to it again. They were all grateful to this Indian girl for saving their lives and helping them along the dangerous Siskiyou Trail. They talked about what they should do with this brave girl. They considered leaving her with some friendly Indian band in the valley if they should meet one. Finally they reached the French Prairie and the Log Inn of Louis Pichette. They asked him what they should do with this girl who had befriended them, as they wanted no harm to come to her and yet none of them wanted to marry her. Louis Pichette told them to leave her with his family and when the Indian Bands would go through in the Spring on their way to their summer camps, he would turn her over to them. But these small tribes would not accept her. Then it was that Louis Pichette took a long straw and broke it into five pieces of different lengths. He told these five men that they should draw straws and the one that drew the longest straw should marry this Indian girl and cautioned them that the one that married her should treat her right as she had saved their lives. It was Adolph Jetti who drew the long straw, so he took this girl for his wife. The other four men each gave her a vial of gold dust for a wedding present in appreciation for what she had done for them. She did not know what to do with this gold so she placed the vials in her husband's hands.

Adolph Jetti took a Land Grant at the Champoeg Landing on the Willamette River. Champoeg had been platted in 1852 and he then built a store on a hill about a half mile from the river and built a new home for his Indian bride, whom he named Julie. He taught her to cook the white man's food that he liked and how to keep house. She learned easily and did her work well, but when it was through she would go to a tepee she had made in the back yard and there she would sit and rest, seemingly happy in her quiet way. However, before many years had passed she died of what was then called "consumption". Adolph Jetti later married again, but it is known that he always treated his Indian bride kindly and held her in high esteem. Adolph Jetti also built the first saloon in Champoeg and that old board building is still standing in this year of 1959.

The other four Frenchmen settled in and around St. Paul. Dieu Donne Manegre bought land from Louis Pichette and built a small house of logs by a spring of pure clear water and near two beautiful creeks. Later, in 1861 he married Emelie, daughter of Louis Pichette and Marguerite Bercier and as their family grew they had need for a larger home so he built a rambling house of good size. Of this marriage they had ten children, I being the youngest of five girls and five boys. . . ."

". . . I was born with an artistic talent that I feel is God-given. I have painted hundreds of pictures in oil and water colors and I also love to paint on china. Thinking back over the years I couldn't begin to count or even remember all the pictures I have painted. I have taught this art work since my children were small and still am at this time. I will paint and create beautiful things as long as I live, and when I am gone my pictures will still live on giving joy to others.

In closing I want to say that I am proud of my Indian strain, also that my forebears helped settle this beautiful Willamette Valley in Oregon. That we are descendants of the first real Americans, the Indian. The Indians considered the white people that came here to be very smart and clever and it is a pity that in their dealings with the Indians that they had not been more fair. If our land was invaded and our homes and food taken from us, we too would fight with our last drop of blood.

I have lived in the Horse and Buggy Age to the Atomic Age and have seen Portland grow from a small town of less than 40,000 to nearly half a million population and in my travels across the United States I have never seen any spot as beautiful as Oregon and in particular the French Prairie in our beautiful Willamette Valley.

Lorraine Wallace Gunnoe"

REMINISCENCES OF HUGH COSGROVE

By H. S. Lyman

(The QUARTERLY of the Oregon Historical Society, Volume I, pages 253, 258-265; 1900)

"Hugh Cosgrove, an Oregon pioneer of 1847, and a representative of the men of some means, who established the business interests of the state, is of Irish birth, having been born in County Cavan, North Ireland in 1811. Although now in his ninetieth year, he is still clear of mind and memory, and recalls with perfect distinctness the many scenes of his active life."

"After making the drive across Iowa and Missouri, in the springtime, when the grass was starting and growing, the Missouri River was crossed, waiting almost a week for their turn at Saint Joe, and then they were west of the Mississippi, with the plains and the Indian country before them. An "organization" was duly effected. Nothing showed the American character more distinctly than the impulse to "organize," whenever two or three were gathered together. It was the social spirit. There was no lack of materials, as besides this party of thirteen families, there were hundreds of others gathering at Saint Joe, the immigration of that year amounting to almost two thousand persons. A train of one hundred and fourteen wagons was soon made up, and Lot Whitcomb was elected captain. Mr. Cosgrove says, "I was elected something. I have forgotten what it was" —but some duty was assigned to each and all, and the big train moved.

Almost immediately upon starting, however, they were met by some trappers coming out of the mountains, who said, "You will never get through that way; but break up in small parties of not over fifteen wagons each.""

It soon proved as the trappers said. The fondness of organization, and having officers, is only exceeded among Americans by the fondness of "going it on one's own hook;" and this, coupled with the delays of the train, broke up Lot Whitcomb's company in two days. In a company, as large as that, a close organization was next to impossible. A trifling break down or accident to one hindered all, and the progress of the whole body was determined by the slowest ox. When Mr. Cosgrove separated his three fine wagons, and active young oxen, and drove out on the prairie, Captain Whitcomb said, "that settles it. If Cosgrove won't stay by me, there is no use trying to keep the company together." With thirteen wagons, and oxen well matched, all went well.

Indians of many tribes were gathered or camped at Saint Joe, and followed the train along the now well traveled road. They were polite as Frenchmen, bowing or tipping their hats, which were worn by some, as they rode along. They expected some little present, usually, but were well satisfied with any article that might be given; and the immigrants expected to pass out a little tobacco or sugar, or some trifle.

There was but one affair with Indians that had any serious side. This occurred at Castle Rock, an eminence out on the prairie, some hundreds of miles from the Mississippi. Here the train was visited, after making the afternoon encampment, by a party of about forty mounted Pawnees, clothed only in buffalo robes. They seemed friendly, asking for sugar and tobacco, as usual. But as they rode off, they disclosed their purpose—making a sudden swoop, to stampede the cattle and the horses of the train. The young men of the train, however, instantly ran for the trail ropes of their horses, and began discharging their pieces at the Indians, who, perhaps, were more in sport than in earnest, or, at least, simply "saucing" the immigrants; and wheeled off to the hills, letting the stock go.

But this was not all of it, as the Pawnees soon overtook two men of the train who were out hunting, and, quickly surrounding them, began making sport, passing jokes, and pointing at the men and laughing to one another; and ended by commanding the alarmed and mystified hunters to take off their clothes, article by article, beginning with their boots. When it came to giving up their shirts, one of the white men hesitated, but was speedily brought to time by a smart stroke across the shoulders by the Indian chief's bow. When the two white men were entirely disrobed, the Pawnees again made remarks, and then commanded them to run for camp; but considerately threw their boots after them, saying they did not want them. Much crestfallen, the two forlorn hunters came out of the hills, "clipping it as fast as they could go" to the train, which was already excited, and thought at first that this was a fresh onslaught of the savages. The men of the train, however, were not very sorry for the young fellows, as they were notorious boasters, and from the first had been declaring that they would shoot, first or last, one Indian a piece before they reached Oregon.

The animal life, as it gradually was encountered, was a source of great interest. The gentle and fleet, but curious, antelopes were the first game. Mr. Cosgrove had two very large and swift greyhounds, which were able to overtake the antelopes. But the meat of these animals was not very greatly relished, being rather dry.

The wolves were the most constant attendants of the train, appearing daily, and howling nightly. These were the large gray wolves, much like our forest species; also, a handsome cream-colored animal, and the black kind, and most curious of all, the variety that was marked with a dark stripe down the back, crossed by another over the shoulders. Then the coyotes were innumerable, and yelped at almost every camp fire. Shooting at the wolves, however, was nothing more than a waste of ammunition, and these animals were at length disregarded. Even the greyhounds learned to let them severely alone, for though at first giving chase ferociously, they soon found a pack of fierce wolves no fun, and were chased back even more ferociously than they started out.

The cities of the prairie dogs were interesting places, and the tiny chirp, a yelp, of the guardian of the door, became a familiar sound. Mr. Cosgrove recalls shooting one of these, finding it much like a chipmunk, only of larger size.

But the great animal of the prairie was the buffalo. The vast herds of these grand animals impressed the travelers of the plains quite differently, almost always giving a shock of strange surprise. One immigrant recalls that his first thought at seeing distant buffaloes, but few in number, in the sparkling distance, was that they were rabbits. With Mr. Cosgrove's party there were indications enough of the animals. Indeed, the plains were strewn with the buffalo chips, and it was the regular thing, noon and evening, as they came to camp, for each man to take his sack and gather enough of them for the camp fire; and coming to the Platte Valley they found the region strewn with the dead bodies of the thousands of animals, which had probably come north too soon, and were caught in the last blizzard of the winter; but no live buffaloes were seen. But at length, as the train crested a slope, and a vast expanse of prairie opened in view, Mr. Cosgrove looked over, and seeing what seemed brown, shaggy tufts thickly studding the distance as far as eye could reach, he exclaimed, "We shall have plenty of firewood now! No need of gathering chips tonight!" He thought the vast Platte Valley was covered with stunted clumps of brush-wood. One of the girls was near, however, and after looking, cried out, "See, they are moving!" Then first he realized it was a herd of buffaloes. Nor were they simply grazing; they were on the run and bearing down on the train. The cry of "buffaloes!" was passed back. It was not altogether safe to be in the path of such an immense herd, and the train was quickly halted, the wagon pins drawn, and a band of hunters quickly went out on horseback to meet the host, and also to get buffalo meat. The herd divided, leaving the train clear and the oxen standing their ground. One part went off to the hills; the other took the fords of the Platte, making the water boil as they dashed through. Enough were shot to stock the train; yet the herd was so vast that at least four hours elapsed before the last flying columns had galloped by—like the last shags of a thundercloud. What a picture—thirteen families with their oxen and wagons, sitting quietly in the midday blaze, while a buffalo troop, perhaps one hundred thousand strong, or even more, dashed past on either side. The best method of preparing the buffalo meat was by jerking it, over a slow fire of sagebrush sticks; the meat being sliced thin, and dried in the smoke in one night. At a later time, when buffalo had become as familiar as cattle, however, the train was stopped by one single monarch. It was just at evening, and the man detailed to go ahead to find a good camping place was out of sight. A shot was heard, however, and the startled train was halted, and the king-pins were drawn, all ready for any emergency; for it might be Indians ahead.

The picket soon was seen, riding at top speed, and crying as he came, "Don't shoot, don't shoot!" and just behind him was an enormous buffalo, charging the whole train. The animal did not stop until within a few rods, and then only with lowered head, and huge square shoulders. The difficulty of shooting him without inducing him to make a charge, if not dropped, was at once apparent. But at length, at a signal, about fifteen rifle balls were poured into his front; and after a moment he began to reel from side to side, and then fell over. Even then no one dared to go and cut the throat, to bleed him; but after a time one cried, "I'll do it!" and the deed was done. It required several yoke of oxen to make a team strong enough to drag him to camp, and his estimated weight was twenty-two hundred pounds.

The last buffalo meat was from an animal that had just been killed by a party of trappers near the divide of the Rocky Mountains. As for deer and elk, none of these were seen on the plains. Birds of the prairie were abundant, especially the sage hens, as the more arid regions were crossed; but the flavor of this fowl was too high for the ordinary appetite. Rattlesnakes were innumerable, but no one of the train suffered from these reptiles except a girl. This occurred at Independence Rock. As the young lady was clambering among the crevices, she incidentally placed her hand upon a snake, which struck. Large doses of whiskey, however, soon neutralized the venom.

After crossing the divide of the Rocky Mountains to the headwaters of the Snake River, the numberless salmon of the streams became the wild food in place of the buffalo meat of the plains. At Salmon Falls there were many Indians of different western tribes taking the fish as they ascended the rapids. In consequence, the royal Chinook was sold very cheap; for a brass button one could buy all that he could carry away. Here occurred a laughable incident. The whole camp was almost stampeded by one wild Indian. He was a venerable fellow, dressed in a tall old silk hat, and a vest, and walked pompously as if conscious of his finery; his clothing, however, being nothing except the hat and vest. At his approach, the camp was alarmed. The more modest hastily retreated to their tents; and some of the men, angry that their wives should be insulted, were for shooting the inconsiderate visitor. A young married man, whose bride was particularly scandalized, was greatly exasperated. But the object of the old Indian was merely peaceable barter. He carried in each hand an immense fish; and Mr. Cosgrove, seeing his inoffensive purpose, bade the boys be moderate, and going out to meet him, hastily sawed a button from his coat, with which he purchased the fish, and sent the old fellow off thoroughly satisfied.

On the Umatilla, after crossing the Blue Mountains, with all their wonders of peak and valley, as they were camped beside the river, the immigrants were visited by Doctor Whitman and his wife, and Mr. and Mrs. Spaulding. Mr. Cosgrove remembers them all very distinctly. Doctor Whitman he describes as tall and well proportioned, of easy bearing, and hair perhaps a little tinged with gray; and very affable. Mrs. Whitman was remarkably fine looking, and much more noticeable than Mrs. Spaulding. Mr. Cosgrove has especial reason to remember the missionaries, because, himself not being well, and this circumstance being discovered by them, he was the recipient of various little delicacies, of fruit, etc., not to be had in the train. A trade was also made between himself and Whitman, of a young cow that had become footsore, and could go no further, for a very good horse. Doctor Whitman, says Mr. Cosgrove, "was a glorious good man;" and the news of his massacre by the Indians a few months later, went over Oregon with a shock like the loss of a personal friend.

Mr. Spaulding gave notice of a preaching service to be held about six miles distant from the camp, and some of the immigrants attended. The coming of the Catholic priests to that region was alluded to in the sermon, and they were spoken of as intruders.

At The Dalles there was a division of opinion among the immigrants as to the best route to follow into the Willamette Valley; whether over the mountains or down the Columbia by bateaux to Vancouver. However, this was easily settled for Mr. Cosgrove's family. Word having reached Vancouver that there were immigrants arriving, bateaux were sent up and in readiness. The price asked for the service was moderate, and the voyage was made quickly and comfortably. The wagons were taken to pieces and loaded upon the boats, and the teamsters had no difficulty in driving the oxen by the old trail, swimming them across the Columbia.

James McKay, a traveling companion, not being able then—though afterwards a wealthy man—to employ a bateaux, built a raft, which brought him through safely. Others went over the mountains.

On arrival at Vancouver, Mr. Cosgrove found a small house, with a big fireplace, which he rented, and housed his family, feeling as happy as a king to be under a roof once more. Here he could leave his family safely while he looked over the country.

By the time that he reached the Cascades, the early autumn rains were falling gently, and at Vancouver they were continuing; but they seemed so light and warm as to cause little discomfort; and the Indians were noticed going around in it unconcernedly barefooted."

EXTRACTS FROM A SPEECH BY U.S. SENATOR JOHN M. GEARIN
Senate of the United States, January 7, 1907
(Last paragraph)

"There are voices calling to us out there—voices of cheer and good will. And we hear them as our fathers heard them on the old emigrant trail—heard them in the noonday sun or in the gathering twilight or under the stars—heard them at the sunrise—borne upon the breezes of the morning from the mountains or from the sea. And we stop at times and listen, and they speak to us of the brotherhood of American genius and American enterprise—a brotherhood of American loyalty and American patriotism, and it strengthens our hearts and cheers us on because we feel that we are brothers all, and that you will listen to us and sympathize with us and aid us—because of that brotherhood."

Author's note: The above paragraph was paraphrased by Senator Gearin's niece, Mary Octavia Murphy, as follows: "Voices from the West are calling. Are you listening?"

FORTY-NINER

The Autobiography of Matthew O'Connell Murphy

"Since the death of my father and mother, I have regretted that I had not been more informed in regard to their family history; and, that my children may not realize the same inconvenience, I have herein endeavored to give such incidents of my life as the infirm memory of my present advanced age will permit.

According to a not very authentic account of my mother, as to date, I was born in Galena, Illinois, June 19, 1830. I am however, of the opinion that the date should be 1829. My grandfather, Andrew Murphy, on my father's side, emigrated to this country from County Wexford, Ireland, A.D. 1799, bringing with him seven children, my father being the youngest and then about 10 years of age; his mother, I think, was dead, or did not survive very long after coming to America. The family took a prominent part in the Wexford disturbance of 1798, and I am inclined to think that the persecution of the English government towards the participants in that revolt was the primary cause of the family's emigration, as my grandfather was in very comfortable circumstances, owning a large estate in Ireland. He located at Galena, Illinois. Owing to the discovery of rich mineral deposits of lead in that vicinity, my father was engaged in his youthful days in those mining industries: when a young man, he attached himself to a surveying party of United States surveyors engaged in sections on the survey of public lands in the vicinity of where now stand the cities of Peoria and Peru, Illinois; subsequently, with a surveying expedition locating a military road in Santa Fe in the Indian Territory, and it was while assisting in these surveys that he acquired a knowledge of that business which he utilized in after life.

I am not certain as to the place or time of the first meeting of my father and mother. My mother's maiden name was Catherine Dillon, and her mother was a Handley of a very respectable family in the City of Clonmel, County Tipperary, Ireland.

My grandmother Margaret Dillon being left a widow with seven children, my mother, fourth in rotation, came with her uncle John Handley to the United States, she (Catherine) being then about 10 years of age, and located in St. Louis, Mo.

Soon after my birth the family moved to New Orleans, where in 1832 my brother Daniel was born. This year was made memorable by the prevalence of yellow fever. My Aunt Mary, a younger sister of my mother, was carried away by that epidemic. At this distant day, I distinctly remember that sad event, the costly funeral and vast throng of mourners. . . .

My father engaged in the boating business soon after going to New Orleans, and it seems, succeeded, for his business assumed vast proportions. I think that when moving to that city the steam boat was wrecked and the family lost their all, barely escaping a watery grave. . . .

In 1837 or '38, the family moved to St. Louis, where my brother William was born, and there is my first recollection of seeing my grandmother; my Aunt Margaret, then a young woman; her brother William and their sister Anne, Mrs. Paulding. The husband of the last was a hatter and doing a large business. I accompanied him out to St. Charles, twenty-nine miles from St. Louis, to visit my Uncle Walter who was a farmer. Leaving there in charge of my grandmother, we took passage on a steamboat for Louisville, Kentucky; and I had to regret the loss of a large coop of game chickens, a present from my Uncle Walter, and which was confiscated by the steward of the steamer while we were stuck on a sand bar, and had run short of meat. My parents had preceded me down the river and my father had purchased in 1838 of one Robert Merriwether a splendid farm eleven miles below Louisville in the same county. This was a very valuable, sightly and highly improved farm situated on the Ohio River. From the house, built on a high bluff, one could see up and down the river; and the vast commerce of the Ohio Valley en route to New Orleans, conveyed by thousands of steam keel and by flatboats, had to pass in full view of the house, nearer than our present abode in Portland (Oregon).

Here, I had my first introduction to school life; and while this was my home, I attended the district school about three miles distant. My time at school was somewhat broken, as a large swamp prevailed in winter between our house and the school; and unless the swamp was frozen over sufficient to bear me up, I had to make a long detour to reach school; this was a sufficient excuse for not going, and many a truant day was spent in the diversions which the swamp afforded when frozen. Moreover, my father every fall loaded two large flat boats with the produce of his farm, consisting of corn, bailed hay, apples, etc., and floated them to New Orleans. This trip occupied about two months, and father's absence, if nothing else, was sufficient for me to induce my mother to consent to my staying from school; so, it cannot be presumed that I made much progress while attending this school. During our stay on the farm, my brother William and infant brother John both died, and my mother prevailed on my father to sell the farm. . . .

. . . When my father sold his farm near Louisville, it was his intention to move to Texas, which had achieved its independence, and was attracting a large emigration. But the vexatious litigation (connected with the sale) and its results seem to have upset his plans, and he started in the fall of 1841 with the family from Louisville, leaving me, then eleven years old, with a friend to forward by next stagecoach to St. Mary's College, a Jesuit institution of great repute, at Lebanon, about sixty miles in the interior. . . .

St. Mary's was a grand institution with twenty-five professors and about two hundred students. The faculty owned a large, highly cultivated farm with a number of slaves of both sexes; numerous lay brothers managed the various departments. The buildings were all of brick, elegant and commodious.

The vacation of 1842 I spent at the College. That of 1843, at the invitation of two of my cousins, pupils of St. Mary's and sons of Major John Handley, at their magnificent plantation in the famous Blue Grass Region of Kentucky. In July, 1844, I was recalled home, bidding adieu to St. Mary's, and at the age of fourteen leaving school, never more to enter as a student.

My father had intended giving me a liberal education; but the vicissitudes of fortune had compelled him to curtail expenses; and thus, was I removed from school at the very time and age that I should have been entering, and ill-prepared to cope with the world. My rewards at the close of my last school year were premiums in Reading, Spelling, Elocution, Geography, Use of the Globes, and Astronomy. I never experienced any trouble in holding my position among classmates. . . .

. . . My father was holding the position of Deputy Sheriff of the County, and I found him occupied at the court house. Mother with brother Dan, Peter and Lucy, twins, whom I had not yet seen were out in the country twenty miles distant. After reaching St. Louis, father had invested what money he had remaining in a steamboat plying on the Illinois River, which proving a success, he purchased the outfit entire and became Captain. Still continuing to make money, he purchased controlling interest in a good boat running on the Missouri and took charge of her, placing his brother-in-law Mr. Paulding in charge of the Illinois boat. Soon thereafter while the latter boat was ascending the river with two barges in tow—and on the fourth of July, 1844, received such damages as stranded father, who, broken up and out of employment was glad to secure a deputy-ship in the Sheriff's office at a small salary, and thus, was I recalled from school. . . .

The sheriff, under whom my father was serving, was defeated, father was thrown out of employment, and I was sent to learn the wagon maker's trade with one John Murphy—no family connection of ours—who conducted a large factory and had made a fortune supplying the government and fur traders with wagons. His wife was a Canadian; and they had no children, and were as mean and miserly as could be. Here I boarded, and every morning at 4 o'clock, I was called and given fifteen cents to go and procure meat for the day, and was kept till 10 o'clock p.m. reading aloud by the light of a dim tallow candle, the life of Martin Luther and other similar works. During the day, I was employed sawing their winter's wood with a bucksaw, turning the grindstone for hours, sometimes painting wagons or wheel-barrows, but generally, catching from the teamster and piling up thousands, if not millions of brick, sufficient to erect a row of brick houses in the spring. My pious, Christian (?) master would not furnish me with a pair of gloves, though my hands were worn raw and covered with blood. The humanity of the teamsters alone saved me from losing my hands entirely, as they would occasionally lend me their gloves. My father was taken violently ill in the latter part of winter and my mother took me home which very much displeased father; and he declared his intention of indenturing me as soon as he recovered. As his illness was very much prolonged, I sought and found employment elsewhere. This is the only instance in which I can now think my father was unreasonably harsh and severe. I can recall times when he became very angry with me but I deserved it, and more.

In the fall of 1844 we moved to St. Louis; and in the fall of 1845 I went into the store of an English cutlery firm, Hancock & Smoot. Mr. Hancock treated me kindly; Smoot was manager of a branch house in Illinois. My duties were such as divolved on boys of that age: opening the store, sweeping, dusting, delivering small packages: the business was not heavy, and all sales by the package. Mr. Hancock and I ran the store, he keeping the books and attending to sales, except an occasional peddler, on whom I would attend.

The firm was winding up the business at the time, and in the spring of '46 closed the house and retired to the store in charge of Smoot. They proposed taking me with them; no doubt, through regard for a favor my father had conferred on them by giving timely warning of the impending failure of a debtor, by which the firm secured payment.

Shortly after, I went into the Hardware Store of Donaldson Hull, a very large establishment with many clerks and one very bright boy about my age who had been two years with the firm, and was familiar with the business which was entirely different from the one I had just left. I suppose I did not suit, for I only retained the place a few months.

When I was discharged my father was greatly displeased, and he shortly after sent me to Murphy's; from whence I entered the carpenter shop of Shook and worked as an apprentice. They employed about twenty men; and here, the knowledge I had gained at John Murphy's in turning the grindstone was put into most constant use; when not so engaged, I was ripping boards, or cleaning shop. In a few months they failed, and Reve Shook, resuming business on a small scale alone, I stayed with him that winter of '46 and into the spring of '47, boarding at home with a small allowance sufficient to clothe and feed me, but which Shook was never able, or willing, to pay me. Here, however, I gained some knowledge of the use of tools, and became pretty expert in laying shingles, flooring, weather-boarding and ordinary framing. Reve soon went under, and I then found employment with a Mr. Abernethy, a sub-contracting carpenter who was finishing one of the finest residences in St. Louis. After a few days' trial, this man told me he would allow me one dollar per day. Most gratifying tidings this was to me: here was an opportunity to make what seemed a fabulous sum, handle some money; heretofore, I had been allowed a mere sufficiency to support life. Mr. Abernethy, however, soon collapsed in business; but he paid me every cent agreed upon, and I found him a kind-hearted, humane, honest man. He was a brother to the first provisional governor of Oregon, and his conversations about that then remote region, created within me a desire to see that land, and forthwith, without the knowledge of my father, I made application to Gen. Fremont then in St. Louis organizing an expedition for exploration in the Oregon Territory; but I was too young, and my application was rejected. I never expected to meet my friend Abernethy, who went West. I did so twenty years after, over on Puget Sound: he then was canvassing Washington Territory as a candidate for Congress; I, prospecting government surveys.

After some intervals of idleness, my father secured a surveying contract for United States government surveys in Southwestern Missouri, and was at that work in the fall and winter of 1845, finishing about Christmas. During his absence, my sister Lucy, aged four and a half years, fell into a cellar of water and was drowned. In the spring of 1846 I went to work for Charles Ryan, a maker of scales; and I remained with him about a year, becoming quite expert in testing and repairing scales. There were two other apprentices in the shop who had been there some time before me. The Ryan Bros. had a large contract to set up corn shellers and agreed to give us fifty cents for each machine. We sat up at night after work hours, and my fellow apprentices agreed to set up one machine each night for me, and to furnish books, on condition that I should read aloud audibly for them. The three machines were completed by midnight, and a large amount of light literature digested. I had now become quite strong; but this night work began to tell on me; I was stricken with inflammatory rheumatism in the spring of 1847, and suffered the greater part of that spring, and never resuming work in the shop. My mother had always opposed this occupation, as working in iron is black, greasy work. In the summer, my aunt Drum, lately bereaved of her husband, came to St. Louis with her son John, and put up with us. Mrs. Drum returned to Galena after a short stay. While in St. Louis her youngest child Mary was baptized, I being sponsor. John remained to doctor his eyes.

After a brief interval, I went into the employment of one Jeffry, a grain broker and storage man. The Mexican War had begun in the fall, and my minority disqualified me from being enrolled as a volunteer. My father was a candidate of the spring election, for City Marshal: there were two Democrats and one Know-nothing in the campaign; the latter was of course elected; the canvass was expensive and my family was involved in very reduced means, the wolf was many times at the door, and I then experienced the greatest poverty ever known in my father's house. The next spring's city elections, the Democrats were successful and B. Mulamphy, a friend of my father, was elected Mayor, and father was tendered the office of Chief of Police; which declining, he was appointed one of three City Weighers—there had been only one before; but the magnitude of the business created such a clamor for the post that to conciliate affairs, three were created, which divided up the proceeds to each; also, led to sharp competition. The salary was regulated by statute; but the business houses had their choice of weighers; each one had about four deputies, and the applicant who could secure the business of the largest dealers secured an appointment, was given the weighing of those houses and received a percentage of his work. John Drum and I were assigned deputy-ships; of course, neither of us could enlarge the business and it was policy for father to have us do all that was not controlled, and I was kept lively when the river was open to navigation.

News of the discovery of gold in California reached us that fall. One of the deputies, Fleming, and one McGowan whom I knew and shall refer to hereafter, immediately started by way of the Isthmus of Panama, and reached the Eldorado that fall. The excitement was intense: every young man that could raise the price of an outfit was determined to go overland in the spring. Cousin Andrew Murphy reached St. Louis that fall. I had never seen him before. Early in the spring our party was organized; Andrew Murphy, John Drum, Tom Murphy—another cousin, James Garvin, O'Connor, a young lawyer, and myself: our individual apportionment was $325, which amount my father gave me. Mr. Jeffry's note for $130 I released to him for five dollars, all that I ever received for six months' service. Our entire outfit—six mules, a wagon, harness and supplies—was shipped by boat from St. Louis to St. Joseph, Mo. We went as passengers, embarking on or about the first of April, 1849. We gave one J. Flynn passage through for his services as driver, at which he was very dexterous with single team, having been a teamster in the Mexican War. Before our departure, however, Andrew and I, about the middle of March started on a brief visitation to our many relatives in and about Galena. We took passage on the first steamboat up the river that spring and made but a short stay. I met in Galena, Aunt Drum and family, Tom O'Leary, a cousin of my father, my Aunt Reed with a large family, a sister of mother's and one or two other relatives. The greater number lived out in the country about twenty miles; but being informed that the roads, owing to the breaking up of winter, were impassable, I did not have the pleasure of seeing a large number of connections. The house where I was born was pointed out, but I did not visit it.

Returning to St. Louis and bidding adieu to my parents —my brother Dan was at Cape Girardeau at school—we started on our overland journey of four months' duration, remaining at St. Joseph about two weeks. We began our tramp on the north bank of the Missouri, and crossed at about where now stand Omaha and Council Bluffs. Although thousands were ahead of us, we found out we were in advance of the growth of the grass on which our animals had to depend; so we engaged a farmer to go with a load of corn about one hundred and fifty miles. We also discovered that we were overloaded and our wagon entirely too heavy; so we purchased a light wagon and four more mules and dispensed with many articles not absolutely necessary. The Missouri crossed, we bid adieu to civilization and plunged into the unknown. We were on the broad, uninhabited plains without a settlement until we reached the gold fields of California, west of the Sierra Nevadas.

We never saw the face of a white man on our long westward journey, except at Forts Laramie, Kearney and Hall, and those of the great throng hastening on, as we were. All were intent and eager to gather up the coveted gold; all seemed impressed with the importance of taking lots of "grub", fearing famine would prevail in that remote region before adequate supplies could reach there to feed the vast multitudes that were congregating there by land and water from every country of the globe. The few exceptions were the wise ones. They distanced the others in the race, brought through their teams in good condition and thereby had a capital to begin with; while the large majority dragged them loaded until they were jaded out and then unloaded on the wayside. Thousands reached the gold fields without animals, provisions or clothing except what was on their person: in the meantime, vessels had come to port laden with provisions and goods of every description, and there was no suffering for supplies in the accessible camps. The first camp we struck was at Weaverville, in Eldorado County, and there we remained mining with butcher-knife and tin pan on the flat about Hangtown some six weeks, during which time we barely made a living. One of the first miners I met was deputy Fleming, who started out from St. Louis at the first news of the discovery of gold, almost a year previous. About the first of October, we left Hangtown for Sacramento very much discouraged with that camp, which soon proved one of the richest in California.

Arriving at Sacramento, I met P. McGowan from St. Louis, established in a wagon repairing shop with a good stock of hard wood, and coining money, having already about $10,000. He was pleased to see me, and proved afterwards a good friend.

Andrew, Drum, Garvin and I concluded to embark with Fred Schatka, a chum of Andrew's from Galena and an uncle of the famous Arctic explorer, and to outfit for a camp known as Gold Run, of fabulous riches. Andrew and Garvin had but little if any money; Drum and I had about $400 and the Schatka man about that amount. A wagon, three yoke of oxen and a load of new supplies to last the winter were purchased, and we were just ready to start when I was taken sick. Drum resolved to nurse me, and we lived in a tent where Sacramento now stands. The others started, and were to let us know where to follow. No mail routes were then established, all were chaos, and we never heard from them until spring. I was not long sick and soon went to work for the Watson Brothers from St. Louis, at sixteen dollars per day, running a cross-cut saw, getting out blocks for a row of stores they were erecting, and finally filling a large ditch, almost a canal, which ran diagonally through their lots, and which had been dug by Colonel Sutter around his fort. John Drum was driving a mule team for some company; but we determined to dig out the gold ourselves, so John and I purchased one little mule and loaded it with our blankets, cooking utensils and provisions and started for

Mariposa Camp in Central California. We had proceeded as far as Angel's Camp, when I was stung by some insect while I was gathering an arm load of wood: my blood being, I suppose, in scurvy condition, my arm became very much inflamed and swollen, and we thought it prudent to return to Sacramento, which we just reached a short time before that city was submerged by the great flood of 1850, when nearly all the inhabitants were forced to seek refuge on a knoll about four miles to the east. Col. Sutter said he had never experienced the like, and it was the greatest rainfall known to that date. When the water subsided, I went to work for McGowan making wagon-beds: here again, my knowledge of the use of carpenter's tools came into play. Drum resumed his old job of mule-driver for the Watson Brothers.

About the first of April, much to our surprise, Andrew and Garvin came down; a snow storm had come upon them before they reached their destination; some of their mules wandered away and were never found; so they erected a cabin and went into winter quarters on the spot. Very good bar diggings were found in the vicinity and they had made about two thousand dollars each, which they insisted should be shared equally with Drum and me, as we had furnished the outfit. We four then went back to the camp where they had wintered and resumed work; but soon discontinued, believing the ground worked out. They had used cradles, and the ground which had four months' handling in that crude system could have been mined over in four weeks with appliances afterwards used. I never saw a sluice box in those days. What was designated as a "long tom" was just coming into use when I left California, one year later.

Most of the gold washing was done with tin pans and wooden bowls, something like our old-fashioned bread bowl; the cradle was a wonderful advance on the first method.

On returning to Sacramento, we dissolved partnership. Garvin, a tinner by trade, went to work in that line; Andrew, as a carpenter; John and I found employment at two hundred dollars per month in the Quartermaster's Department of a government expedition under command of General Nathaniel Lyons, afterwards killed in the Civil War at Pea Ridge. Lieutenant Stoneman, afterwards Governor of California, was an officer in the same expedition.

. . . We crossed the Sierra Nevada Mts. from the head of the Sacramento at the base of Mt. Shasta and journeyed to Goose Lake in Oregon. The objects of this expedition were first to recover the effects "cached" the previous fall by some United States expedition, and to inter the remains of a U.S. Engineer who had been murdered by savages; second, to afford protection to such emigrants as should seek to come into California on this northern route. . . .

We did supply some starving emigrants with food, saw the remains of others who had been killed by the Indians, but the Indians kept out of sight and harm's way . . ."

THE STORY OF
MARY ELLEN COSTELLO

By Mary Ellen (Costello) Murphy

"My mother, Ellen Burns, was one of eight children of John Burns of West Meath County, Ireland, the others being her five brothers—Patrick, James, Hugh, Lawrence and Daniel—and her two sisters—Mary and Margaret.

Uncle James, who had learned navigation, sailed to America and sent for his young sister Ellen to join him. On the voyage across the Atlantic, she met a young countryman, John Costello, who came from the bordering County of Meath, where he had sold shoes, but in common with many in troubled Ireland, had determined to seek a new life in the new world.

On her arrival in Baltimore, young Ellen learned that her brother's vessel had been captured by the notorious pirate, Gibbs, and that her brother James had been killed in the struggle for the ship. Alone and friendless except for her fellow-passenger, Ellen refused kindly offers of aid to return to her family in Ireland, and resolving to remain in this new, growing country, found employment in Baltimore with the wife of an army officer.

Her shipboard friend, John Costello, soon established himself and claimed Ellen as his bride. They lived in Baltimore for a few years, and there my brother James and my sister Mary Ann were born, after which the family moved to Fort Wayne, Indiana, where they ran a hotel in the old Council House, a two-story log structure, with a main stairway connecting the two portions of the building. In this historic spot had been held the councils between the Territorial Governor, and the leaders of the Indian tribes.

In addition to running a hotel, my father trucked supplies into Michigan by wagon, prospering from these joint enterprises.

The family increased in size, with four more children being born in Fort Wayne—John, then myself, Mary Ellen, in 1836, then Eliza Ann who died at birth, and Michael, who died many years later in Oregon.

To provide a more suitable home than the hotel for his wife and children, Father bought two tracts of timbered land to start a farm. The strenuous work of felling the huge trees and clearing the land for the plow so undermined Father's health that he died, about 1847, leaving Mother with us five children.

I was then about ten years old and in school—a district school which was held for only three months during the winter. Later, when I was about thirteen, I was sent, for a year, to boarding school at the Convent of Notre Dame, in Fort Wayne, where I suffered greatly from homesickness, and was eager to return home.

Mother's cares on the farm were very heavy for her, even with our help, and early in 1849 she married John Gearin, a neighboring farmer, whose wife and mother of his five children had died five years before.

That Spring my oldest brother James left home, crossing the plains to seek for gold in California. In October, my half-brother was born and named Hugh Burns, after Mother's brother, who with Uncle Lawrence, was out in the Oregon Territory. They were then working in Oregon City in the blacksmith and carpentering trades at a fabulous daily wage of eight dollars.

Their letters were so glowing with enthusiasm over the opportunities in Oregon and their urging that we come West so insistent, that Mother grew restless, particularly with so many others planning to leave. So Mother and Mr. Gearin made plans to leave for this new fruitful land. Mr. Gearin disposed of his farm to his oldest son Cornelius, and in May of 1851 the family, Mr. Gearin, Mother and us five children, joined the throng of emigrants to Oregon.

Leaving Fort Wayne in March, we went down the canal to Cincinnati, Ohio and taking the steamer "Bay State", embarked for St. Joseph, Missouri, from which point the real journey of "crossing the plains" began. Our outfit comprised six yoke of oxen, five cows and an emigrant wagon built like a boat, with a water-tight bottom. Loaded on the wagon were our supplies, with sufficient food for six months, consisting of flour, bacon, rice, beans, coffee and tea, sugar and dried apples, with seasoning and condiments. Our train was composed of twenty-five or thirty wagons. Tim Davenport and his brother, both young men, were in our train, as were the sister and brother-in-law of Governor Thurston. Very few young single women were in the party—mostly young married folk with small children, with young men as drivers.

At the end of our first day's journey all civilization was left behind and, except for Forts Laramie and Hall, we did not see a settlement until we reached The Dalles in Oregon. Breaking the cattle to drive was very difficult, but our cows gave us a needed supply of good milk.

We were not permitted to kill any game, or birds, for fear of alarm to the Indians. I remember the terror of the elders because of the Indians and I recall one night as I sat in the wagon, seeing an Indian stealing along outside the lines. In about ten minutes the report of his gun warned us that he had found a victim, who proved to be one of the young men in the train ahead, who died from the effects of the poisoned bullet. Mother had put in a supply of beads, tobacco and small trinkets, and by giving these, no harm came to our immediate train.

The trains were an endless source of interest to the Indians, and privacy was an utter impossibility, as they would surround the camps at night and peer with curiosity into each wagon, or watch the preparations for the meals. A small amount of sugar given them was a delight and even the smallest amount was shared with the others, regardless of numbers. A pipe of tobacco was also shared similarly. One evening as I stood with my little sister, a chief of the Pawnee tribe watched me, and after some time went up to my stepfather, Mr. Gearin, and offered him forty Indian ponies for me. When asked why he wanted me, he replied, "For my son's wife."

I had a fear thereafter of being stolen, and never left the train but once, when I was riding a horse and not realizing the slowness of the others with the wagon train, rode on, far ahead, thrilled with being a part of this great adventure and day dreaming of the future, when realization of my peril came to me. I feared to return through the great waste of the plains and low hills, with no sight or sound of civilization around me, while the knowledge that at any moment an Indian might appear and carry me away, struck me with terror. I knew by the appearance of the sun that it was growing toward evening. Frightened, I crawled under a shelving rock and, holding the reins of my horse, waited tremulously for fully three hours until I heard the welcome noise of the slow-moving wagons.

All of the trains were warned of the hostility of the Snake River Indians, as they were reported to be the most warlike of all the tribes.

In all our journey I can recall travelling only once during the night, and the spot is forgotten, but to cross in safety it was necessary to go through in the cool of the night, which we did after having rested the oxen and cattle for some hours.

We passed through many deserted Indian villages but saw few Indian women during the trip. Thousands of Indians were in conclave at Fort Laramie when we arrived there. The women wore blankets, but the men, brown, large and muscular, and generally carrying a bow and arrows, were clothed in moccasins and a breech cloth. Quills in the hair and ornaments, always served as a guide to those of greatest consequence in the tribe.

Each night as we pitched tents we were always facing the setting sun. I recall seeing no buffalo, but for fuel I many times gathered the chips for our little reflector stove. The teakettle would boil on top and the bread bake on each side by the aid of these reflectors. At night the women would bake bread and prepare food for the next day. Often my mother would bake the whole night long to prepare food for the weary, hungry ones of our wagon. Always the young men served as guards during the night to prevent the Indians from causing a stampede of the cattle. We had no trouble from this source, but great inconvenience was caused and long delays were met in finding and rounding up the stock. The weather was favorable except when we reached the River Platte, where we encountered a severe hail storm, when the hail, as large as hen's eggs, fell to a depth of several inches. This storm caused the only stampede on our journey. The cattle were beaten terribly and the men suffered in their endeavor to recover them.

Our Ascent of the Rockies was not apparent and no more inconvenience was caused than the occasion would demand. The cattle at times became unmanageable, wagons would be turned over, streams had to be crossed. At times as long as two days would be required to cross a wagon train over a river. The running gear of the wagon had to be taken apart and placed in the schooner bed which, serving as a boat, was floated to the other side. When all the wagons were so crossed, the cattle and horses had to be driven into the river to swim across. The current of the swift streams would carry some of them far down the river and the men would have to labor strenuously to recover them and drive them back upstream to the wagons.

Nearing the West, a few ferries were met. I recall the first, on the Snake River. . ."

EXCERPTS FROM THE CHRONICLES OF THE HOUSE OF ST. PAUL
Sisters of the Holy Names, July 2, 1872

The young ladies of the Academy of Saint Paul, Marion Co., Ore., had their annual examination on the first day of July. They went through all the branches from Spelling to Algebra and Astronomy, in a way highly creditable to themselves and to their teachers. On the next day they had their exhibition and according to the testimony of all those who were present, it was a complete success. It began with a lively march on the piano and harmonium. Miss Mary Weston delivered the salutatory in her usual easy and graceful manner. Then various pieces were either played, sung or read by the students, Miss Eliza Coleman, Miss Katie McKay, Miss Minnie Murphy and Miss Anna Kennedy, with several others exhibiting therein some fine specimens of their acquirements. A drama entitled "Coronation of Isabelle I" came next and lasted two hours. Miss Anna Kennedy, Miss Agnes Nibler and Miss Emma Coleman, in the capacity of Performance Managers, gave each a preliminary address on the said subject. Two prologues followed. The first one was delivered in a good humored and most exquisite manner by Miss Anna Kennedy, acting the part of History, Miss Minnie Murphy, under the personification of Spain, recited the second, and raised feelings of sympathy by her pathetic narrative. The four acts of the drama were then performed in a way which kept the large audience enraptured to the very last. Miss Mary Weston, in the role of the Directress of the convent of Alamanca displayed the tempered firmness suiting the Superior of a great establishment, the wisdom of an experienced counsellor and the heart-felt love of a mother. Miss Albina Graton, as Sister Angela had the calm gentleness of a devoted teacher. Miss Eliza Coleman excited general admiration by the bold and masterly style of her performance. After being haughty and despotic, while standing on the summit of grandeur she won the pity of all by her humble resignation under the chastisement which crushed her brightest hopes. Miss Katie McKay, representing the part of the real Isabelle, manifested the meek fortitude of a true Christian under the pressure of adversity, the enthusiastic patriotism of a crusader for the welfare of her native land, and the sublime magnanimity of a queen whose motto was: Justice, Love and Clemency.

Miss Elizabeth Brummel, in the character of a far-seeing adviser gave with a proper solemness, the most wholesome counsels and warnings. Miss Emma Paterson appeared as a warm comforter of the distressed and as one who after having undauntedly offered rebuke to a friend in prosperity, never forsakes the name in misfortune. Miss Mary Lambert illustrated, in a very impressive manner, the anguish felt by a guilty conscience and the happiness obtained by a true conversion. Miss Dorilda Gagnon and Miss Leonie Paterson acting as cousins of Dona Isabelle fulfilled their parts with great ease and the real accent of nature. Miss Rosalie Sweeney, personifying the High Chancellor displayed the fine manners of a Christian Lord and the fine manners of a Christian. Miss Bridget McDonald, as nurse to the princess, as Miss Sydonia Sweeney, for her daughter, elicited great sympathy by the effusion of motherly love which she bestowed on one she had wronged. Miss Salomie Raymond, in the garb of a poor blind girl, and her sister, Miss Magdalen Raymond, drew tears from many eyes by their sweetly sung lays and the tender affection they professed for each other. Miss Mary Hunt, as the door keeper of the convent, and Ellen Coffey as the chief cook of the establishment, delighted their hearers in another way; for many a hearty laugh they elicited by their humorous sayings. Finally, the following young ladies, Ellen McDonald, Rose Allard, Margaret Marshal, Teresa Nibler, Esther Jackson, Victoria Graton, Zenaide Gregoire and Marcelina Gervais—playing as pupils of the Academy of Salamanca, merited likewise the applause of the listening throng by their artless language, joyous shouts and suitable demeanor. Besides the beauty of the entertainment all noticed the moral of the drama. Indeed many important teachings were exemplified therein and every sentence was an instruction. When the representation was ended, the distribution of premiums took place and the happy students received the rewards of the Academic labors in the satisfaction enjoyed by their beloved parents.

Miss Elizabeth Brummel offered the valedictory address in a feeling tone, and Very Reverend B. Delorme, pastor of the place, closed the exhibition by a few words of felicitation and encouragement. Very Reverend J. F. Fierins, and Reverend P. McCormick of Portland, honored by their presence the joyful manifestation. I will not conclude this short and imperfect report without stating that the Academy of Saint Paul, thanks to the skillful administration of its highly esteemed Sister Superior and the zealous spirit of the teachers, has proved to be a valuable institution to the country and to make known this appreciation is to express a public sentiment.

EXTRACTS FROM A LETTER WRITTEN BY JAMES MARTIN TO MARY McKAY in 1892

(James Martin, Sr. had visited his son, James Martin, Jr., a cousin of Mrs. James McKay, who came to Oregon about 1870 and stayed for about 30 years in the St. Paul area with the McKays and the McCormicks.)

"   Ballinasloe, Ireland
Dear Cousin Mary:

. . . While in London I intended taking a run down to Kent to see the Hop Industry, but I did not have the opportunity. I wanted to see how they manage in England and find out what the prospects were. From what I learned at the Hop Exchange though, I find the crop is good and excellent in quality. It then wanted a few weeks of picking season, and since then it has rained very heavily every day, and I should imagine it would do some damage. But the summer has been very dry and fine, and I have no doubt the season's crop will be a good turnout. Thousands of the poor people of London had gone out to the yards a month in advance so as to be employed when the picking began, and before I left I was shown crowds of them returning destitute and hungry, as the wet wintry weather had almost drowned them out. I wonder what are the Oregon hop prospects. What a bad time they had last year with regard to price. Did Will (McKay) and John (McKay) get anything at all? I am sure a great number of growers have neglected their yards this year. These fine Hop Houses stand as a bad monument to a bad enterprise that must have ruined many a farmer. . .

So the bad times prevented all the prospective weddings from taking place around St. Paul. That was indeed sad news, but perhaps by this time both Laura and Jennie Davidson have entered the blissful state of matrimony, and darling Zelia (Davidson) contemplating a like issue. How is my old and particular friend Mrs. Cooke? Well and happy as usual I have no doubt. She was always very kind to me whenever I called and if she were nearer I would gladly send her a bottle of genuine "poteen" as a remembrance of the many pleasant social visits I made at her mansion. Mary (Cooke) is still unmarried I presume.

Old Mr. Kirk reminds me of a cat with many lives. With all the accidents and sicknesses he has had, he ought to have been dead many years ago. But without wishing him any ill luck, I hope he is still living and that he got over the painful operation you described. Kindly remember me to him. I suppose you hardly ever see Father Blanchet now that he has removed to Gervais. I daresay he is as well as usual and not much changed.

I hope Will's (McKay) family are all well. I fancy the boys must be grown big fellows by now and able to lend their father a helping hand. Did Mrs. Kavanaugh ever come to Ireland as she expected? I would have gladly gone to see her and perhaps might have induced her to come to Ballinasloe for a visit. I suppose Mrs. Tom Coleman is the same as ever and keeps as nice a flower garden as she used to. Your father, I suppose he is still well and able to attend to business, with John of course to help him. Is he still living in town or does he spend most of his time now in the country? I shall expect to have an answer to this letter in due course, but I know I don't deserve one for being so long in writing you. Must make an effort to write to John McCormick next.

All Kind Regards   Believe me   Your affect. Cousin
James Martin"

BIBLIOGRAPHY

Bagley, Clarence B., *Early Catholic Missions in Oregon*, Lowman and Hanford, Seattle, Washington, 1932

Bancroft, Hubert Howe, *History of Oregon*, The History Company, San Francisco, 1888

Chapman Publishing Company, *Portrait and Biographical Record of the Willamette Valley, Oregon*, Chapman Publishing Company, Chicago, 1903

Clark, Robert Carlton, Ph.D., *History of Willamette Valley, Oregon*, S.J. Clarke Publishing Co., Chicago, 1927

Corning, Howard McKinley, *Dictionary of Oregon History*, Binford and Mort, Portland, Oregon, 1956

Corning, Howard McKinley, *Willamette Landings*, Binford and Mort, Portland, Oregon, 1947

Dobbs, Caroline, *Men of Champoeg*, Metropolitan Press, Portland, Oregon, 1932

Dominica, Sr. Mary, S.N.D., *Willamette Interlude*, Pacific Books, Palo Alto, California, 1959

Garraghan, Gilbert, *Jesuits in the Middle United States, Volume II*, America Press, New York, 1938

Gaston, Joseph, *Centennial History of Oregon*, S.J. Clarke Publishing Co., Chicago, 1912

Geer, T.T., *50 Years in Oregon*, The Neale Publishing Co., New York, 1912

Lang, Herbert O., *History of the Willamette Valley*, Himes & Lang, Portland, Oregon, 1885

Mercer, A.S., *Marion County, Oregon*, State of Oregon, Salem, Oregon, 1876

Nichols, Leona, *Mantle of Elias*, Binford and Mort, Portland, Oregon, 1941

O'Hara, Edwin V., *Pioneer Catholic History of Oregon*, Glass & Prudhomme, Portland, Oregon, 1911

Parrish, P.H., *Historical Oregon* (Revised Edition), The Macmillan Co., New York, 1949

Schoenborg, Wilfred P., S.J., *Jesuits in Oregon*, Oregon Jesuit, Portland, Oregon 1959

West, Oswald, *Story of French Prairie*

Newspapers:
Oregon Spectator, Oregon City, Oregon
Oregon Journal, Portland, Oregon
Oregon Statesman, Salem, Oregon
The Oregonian, Portland, Oregon
Portland Telegram, Portland, Oregon

Periodicals:
Catholic Sentinel, Portland, Oregon
Champoeg Pioneer, Aurora, Oregon
Marion County History, Salem, Oregon
Oregon Historical Society Quarterly, Portland, Oregon
Oregon Farmer, Salem, Oregon
St. Joseph's Magazine, Mt. Angel, Oregon
Willamette Farmer, Salem, Oregon

Archives and related:
California State Archives, Sacramento, California
Oregon State Archives, Salem, Oregon
Latter Day Saints Genealogical Research Library, Los Angeles, California
Ben Maxwell Card Index, Salem, Oregon
Sacramento County Historical Society, Sacramento, California
Oregon Historical Society, Portland, Oregon

Other sources:
Chronicles of the House of St. Paul, 1860-1890
    Sisters of the Holy Names, Marylhurst, Oregon
"St. Paul's on the Willamette", 1834-1849,
    by Sister Mary Agnesia Murphy, S.N.J.M.
    Crosby Library, Gonzaga University, Spokane, Washington
Historical Outline St. Paul's Rectory, 1839-1946
Personal records, autobiographies, reminiscences, diaries, letters, notebooks, news articles and pictures of thirty-two families whose ancestors settled in the St. Paul, Oregon area between 1820 and 1890, and pertinent conversations and correspondence.
Land maps and various official records of Marion County, the State of Oregon, and the Catholic Archdiocese of Portland, Oregon.
Personal and family records.

INDEX

Northwest Fur Company, 1, 3, 4, 5, 7, 94, 149, 151, 156
Notre Dame University, 57, 124, 187
Nouete, Josephite, 5, 101

Oahslager, Henry, 71
Oats, 8, 19, 50, 95, 117, 135, 147, 176
O'Connor, Martha J., 176
Ogden, Peter S., Dr., 114
Okanogan, Josephite, 7, 183
Okanogan, Suzanne, 153
Olds, Wortman & King, 52
O'Neill, Mr., 135
OREGANO, S.S., 79
Oregon-California Railroad, 61, 71
Oregon City Falls, 9, 33, 44, 50
Oregon City Locks, 66
Oregon City, Oregon, 9, 13, 17, 18, 19, 20, 23, 27, 28, 29, 30, 32, 36, 37, 46, 51, 57, 59, 81, 110, 114, 177, 179
Oregon Country, 1, 5, 8, 9, 11, 12, 13, 15, 16, 18, 19, 20, 24, 27, 28, 30, 77, 95, 102, 109, 113, 123, 153
Oregon Country missions, 11, 13
Oregon, eastern, 24, 102, 138
Oregon legislature, 125, 162, 187
Oregon Pioneer Association, 151
Oregon School Bill, 138
Oregon, State of, 43, 44, 87
Oregon Supreme Court, 71
Oregon Territory, 31, 95, 110, 167
Oregon Trail, 28
Oregon, University of, 127
Oregon Volunteer Army, 22, 24, 33, 96, 109, 150
Oregonian Railway Co., Ltd., 69
Organ, 184
O'Reilly, Father, 41
Orphanages, 66, 171
Orton, Caledonia, 65, 106, *also see* Coleman, Thomas, Mrs.
Orton, Ira, Mr. and Mrs., 66
Oxen, 105, 124, 130, 134, 136, 140, 159, 161, 164

Pacific Fur Co., 1
Pacific Northwest, 30, 31, 50, 87
Pacific Ocean, 1, 5
Panama, Isthmus of, 46, 56, 65, 119, 137, 169, 173, 186
Paramount Pictures, Inc., 121
Paris, 12

Parties, house, 56, 65, 66, 75, 103, 106, 124
Parties, riding, 56, 57
Passenger boats, 17
Pasture, 41
Paterson, Emma, 63
Paterson, Leonie, 63
Paul, Apostle, 11
Payne, Mr., 184
Pearl Harbor, Hawaii, 87
Peavey, logging, 89, 154
Pegs, wooden, 41
Peletier, S., 71
Pelland, Charles A., 81, 87
Pelland, Charles O., 58, 63, 75, 78, 106, 177, 178
Pelland, Charles O., Mrs., 75, 177, 178
Pelland, Florence, 178
Pelland, Fred J., 178
Pelland, George, 178
Pelland, Gerald, 178
Pelland, Helen, 178
Pelland-Larocque Store, 58, 59, 61, 68, 131, 132, 177
Pelland, Marie, 178
Pelland, Philip, 178
Pelland's Store, 75, 78, 178
Pembrooke, Mr., 162
Perrault, Jean, 8
Perrault, Mary Ann, 8
Piano, 61, 217
Picard, Andre, 42, 150
Picard, Emilie, 42, 150
Picard, Henri, II, 75, 103
Picard, Honore (Henri), 37, 71, 102
Picard, Jewell, 103
Picard, John, 103
Picard, Salome, 75
Pichet, Catherine, 152, *also see* Lambert, Augustin, Mrs.
Pichet, Emelie, 47, 156, *also see* Manegre, DieuDonne, Mrs.
Pichet, Louis, 7, 32, 36, 47, 131, 156, 189-193
Pichet, Marguerite, 32
Pichet, Marguerite (Bercier), 32
Pichet's Log Inn, 32, 44, 131, 156, 191, 192
Piette, F., 59
Piette, J. B. P., 71
Piette, Mr., 191
Pillette, Herman, 81, 86

THE AUTHOR

Harvey James McKay was born and raised in St. Paul, Oregon where all of his great-grandparents settled between 1847 and 1870. He graduated from St. Paul High School and the University of Portland.

After the outbreak of World War II he enlisted in the Army Air Corps. He eventually became an Air Corps Officer and was the Adjutant of the Air Force headquarters that made the major landings in the South Pacific Theatre of Operations. Later, as an Air Force civilian employee, he was the Air Force Monitor for the Air Force-Industry Cost Reduction Program. In 1960 he received the Air Force Association's National Medal of Merit.

In 1976 he was a member of the Brown-for-President Campaign Staff and was a member of the California Delegation at the Democratic National Convention.

Mr. McKay is a retired U.S. Civil Service employee and a retired Air Force Lt. Colonel and lives in Glendale, California.